# ISLANDS OF ESSEX

## Ian Yearsley

Ian Henry Publications

**Second edition**

ISBN  0 86025 509 3

The cover photograph
is of the Oyster Pits
on Packing Sheds Island

Published by
Ian Henry Publications, Ltd.
20 Park Drive, Romford, Essex RM1 4LH
and printed by
Whitstable Litho
Millstrood Road, Whitstable, Kent CT5 3PP

# PREFACE

The success of the first edition of *Islands of Essex* took everyone by surprise - including the author! The feeling that there was something magical about island life was obviously something that was widely shared.

The first edition did little more than bring together everything that had previously been published about Essex islands - there was a myriad of information available, but no central reference work. My intention with that edition was simply to bring all that information together.

This new edition is still based on that original concept, but a new approach has been taken and the book now benefits from the addition of several new features. More original research has been carried out and a lot of new material has consequently come to light. A few corrections and clarifications have been made to the text of the original book and there is a new, easier-to-follow, structure which orders the islands in geographical terms as if one were taking a logical journey around them up the coast.

There is also a lot of new content arising from changes to the islands themselves. Canvey Island, for example, has seen new road and retail developments and new housing. Foulness has seen changes to its Ministry of Defence presence as the post-Cold War years have led to a reduction in military activity.

I have also extended the remit of the book to include a handful of the more significant off-shore marshland areas that probably qualify as islands in their own right. This makes the book even more definitive as *the* Essex island reference source. I have enjoyed updating the book for this new edition. It has brought home to me how much information there was in the original and has enabled me to build upon that content to produce an even better book with this revised edition. It has also given me the opportunity to revisit the islands and rediscover the enthusiasm for them that I felt when carrying out my research for the first book.

I said in the first edition that island life held a strange fascination for me and it is evident from the letters I have received in response to it that this fascination is shared by many Essex people. I hope you enjoy reading this new, updated edition of *Islands of Essex* and continue to take the chance of visiting Essex islands whenever that opportunity arises.

2

## ACKNOWLEDGEMENTS

I would like to make several acknowledgements...

First and foremost, I would like to thank Ian Wilkes for his confidence in me with the first edition of the book and for his enthusiasm and encouragement for this second edition.

I would also like to thank the following for their help specifically with this new edition: Mr. J. Backhouse (Horsey); G. W. Booker, Oikos Storage Ltd. (Canvey); Denise Carr (Foulness); Colchester Oyster Fishery (Pewit, Rat and Cindery); Mr. & Mrs. Cole (Osea); R. W. Crump, B.E.M. (Foulness); Essex Wildlife Trust/Ray Marsh (Skipper's); Exchem Organics (Bob Thomas, Brian Campbell, Pat Heaney) (Bramble); Major A. S. Hill, retired (Foulness); Sharon Hume (Foulness); Mersea & Tollesbury Oyster Fishery (Mersea); Harry Paar (Bridgemarsh); Peter G. Philpot (Potton); Doug Powell (Mersea and the smaller islands in the Mersea locality); Paul Schofield, COMAX/DERA (Foulness); Dave Smith, Meteorological Office (Canvey); June Thompson, Community Safety & Emergency Plans, Essex County Council (Canvey); and Richard Wallace/National Trust (Northey).

The Strood causeway leading to Mersea Island (in the background)

# INTRODUCTION

*"It is wonderful how much the interest of a piece of land is augmented by the simple fact of its being surrounded with water."*

PHILIP HAMERTON, *Paris*

*"I doubt, indeed, if there is any man of understanding who has not desired an island, a sea-encircled dab on the map?"*

JAMES WENTWORTH DAY, *Coastal Adventure*

There has always been something magical about islands, though quite what the source of this magic is is difficult to define. Perhaps it is the very adventure involved in getting to them, since most cannot be easily approached on foot or by car in the way that one might approach an 'ordinary' piece of mainland. Perhaps it is their remoteness, their isolation, their sense of timelessness - characteristics which are emphasised by the fact that most of them, due in no small part to the difficulty inherent in attaining them, remain largely unspoilt by human residential habitation. Or perhaps the magic springs solely from the special place they occupy in our hearts from the days of schoolroom literature, where treasure-seeking pirates, survivors of shipwrecks and bands of amateur teenage sleuths out for an adventure were two-a-penny.

In former days many of our islands were working places where fishermen and farmers toiled at their businesses for long hours and the creeks around them were home to gangs of smugglers who risked their lives to bring in cargoes of liquor, perfume and textiles under the noses of the revenue officers. Now they are mainly centres of leisure and recreational activity, visited by yachtsmen, artists and naturalists and Sunday afternoon strollers out to take the air. In the hectic, bustling world of the early 21st century, they are, quite literally, places where one can 'get away from it all'.

It has been claimed that there are some 5,000 pieces of land in the British Isles which could be classified as islands. But this fantastic number is constantly changing as the actions of the wind and the tides erode and swamp some areas of land whilst building up deposits to form new areas in other places. The Shetlands, the Orkneys and the Hebrides account for about 700 of this 5,000 total, while countless other familiar names and shapes, such as those of the Channel Islands, the Scilly Isles, the Isle of Wight, the Isle of Man and Anglesey, spring readily to mind.

Even in Essex, a handful of islands can be called to mind almost immediately - Canvey, Foulness and Mersea are the most obvious - but as almost the entire length of the county's coastline is punctuated by inlets, or, more precisely, outlets, of creeks and rivers, interspersed with low-lying marshland and saltings, it is not hard to appreciate why the very fragmented nature of this landscape produces an off-shore panorama which encompasses something like 30-40 islands in all. Surprisingly, this equates to more islands than all the counties in the rest of eastern England can manage put together.

The *Guinness Book of Records* once claimed that there were a mere 1,031 genuine islands in Britain, of which the UK mainland, itself the eighth largest island in the world, is clearly the biggest. The vast difference in number between this total and that claimed above serves well to illustrate one of the great difficulties in the 'sport' of island hunting - the apparent non-existence of a satisfactory, established definition of what exactly constitutes an island.

Kenneth Strugnell, in *Seagates to the Saxon Shore,* ventures to suggest that it must include skerries, which are sizeable rock formations exposed only at certain states of the tide, but is at a loss to determine whether this also includes "mere sandbanks". He is equally unhappy to apply the definition to areas of land which are "encircled by water so confined in its channels" that they are considered to be islands almost by default. In Essex, where the marshland coastline is by its very nature both low-lying and constantly changing, there are many areas of land which could be counted as islands simply because they protrude a few feet above the water at high tide, whilst the surrounding matter lies a similar distance below the surface. There is much also, notably in the so-called Essex Archipelago at the confluence of the Rivers Crouch and Thames, which fits readily and happily into the last of Strugnell's categories, though the case for considering that the six raised areas of land which occupy this curious and remote corner of the county are not anything other than islands is surely an extremely tenuous one.

Taking this to extremes, one could argue the point indefinitely. What about the inland islands, like those on the lake at Gosfield, on the reservoirs at Hanningfield and Walthamstow and in the gravel pits at Fingringhoe Wick (to name but a few) - are these to be included also? Ignoring the frivolity, the point is surely taken.

Trying to finalise an exact count of islands at any time would prove to be a difficult operation. This is partly because no-one is really too sure exactly what should or should not be included and partly because the coastline is constantly changing. A trip around the British Isles in an attempt to draw up a definitive island catalogue would be an exercise akin to that of painting the Forth Bridge - once the job was done it would have to be begun again almost immediately.

The shape of the Essex coastline, in terms of both the mainland and the islands, has changed dramatically in the centuries since the last Ice Age, settling down roughly to its present form during the Mesolithic period (c.4500 BC). The rise in sea levels as a result of the ice melting led to much former mainland being submerged - some new islands sprang up where once dry land had been, whilst others disappeared altogether.

Since then, other natural factors have also played a significant part in shaping the Essex coastline. The cliffs at Walton-on-the-Naze have suffered heavily from coastal erosion, retreating a great distance inland over the centuries with, amongst other things, the loss of the town's original parish church to the sea in 1798. In addition, severe flooding has taken place all along the coast with alarming regularity over the past few hundred years, resulting in the loss of much land to the sea. Some of these floods, notably those of 1736, 1897 and 1953, affected many areas, particularly along the Thames coastline. The introduction of sea defences from the 18th century onwards was a step in the right direction towards checking the advance of the sea, but even into this century seawalls were invariably inadequately maintained, as there was initially no overall body responsible for their upkeep, and many of them soon fell into disrepair.

It was the traumas of the First World War which really brought home the importance of flood defences and the need to cling on to all available agricultural land, as the threat to British shipping from German submarines meant that the country became increasingly reliant upon the need to produce its own food. Even so, it was not until 1928, when London was flooded, that the Government took any positive steps towards the introduction of a national and unified approach to sea defences. The Woolwich Barrier was still half a century away.

Today, the risk of flooding, though not as great as in the past due to the introduction of modern seawalls, still remains an ever-present threat in some areas. In Essex, a county whose islands are almost exclusively low-lying marshland areas, island inhabitants pay particular attention to the storm tide warnings of the weathermen. Fifty years on from the devastation of Canvey, an innate fear of the sea has still not receded.

Though in some places much land has been lost to the sea over the years, much has also been reclaimed from it in other areas. The climate in Essex has proved very favourable for arable farming and for the rearing of livestock and the rich coastal marshland of which most of the county's islands are made has therefore developed a significant agricultural value. Numerous reclamations of extremely fertile areas of land have consequently taken place up and down the coast.

The origins of land reclamation are difficult to date but are known to have taken place in some areas from at least 1280. Most of this reclamation, including about four-fifths of that carried out at Foulness Island, was completed by 1500. After that there were relatively few successful large reclamation schemes undertaken, a notable exception being the Dutch reclamation of Canvey Island in the 1620s. Even so, land reclamation was still a popular issue well into the 19th century as the demands of an ever-increasing urban population led to a continual search for more and more crop-growing acreage, but the developments proposed and effected at this time were relatively small-scale in comparison. This thirst for expansion even continues into modern times. At major population centres like Southend, where land is in short supply as the town is hemmed in on the landward sides by the Green Belt, reclamation of the foreshore is a recurring option put forward by developers - but for residential and leisure purposes, not for agricultural ones.

It is worth noting, however, that not all schemes for land reclamation have been a success. The failure of the Maplin Airport project in the 1970s is the most recent and most obvious example of this. The successful construction of a brand new island in the sea supporting an international airport would have been a quite remarkable civil engineering achievement but the much-publicised opposition to this proposal finally won the day and the project, let alone the aeroplanes, never left the ground. Before that, in the 19th century, a remarkably similar if vast and unwieldy plan by the South Essex Estuary and Reclamation Company to reclaim land off Maplin Sands, Foulness Sands, Ray Sand, Dengie Flats and St Peter's Sands, this time for agricultural purposes, also failed to get the necessary moral and financial support.

It is clear, though, that the practice of land reclamation and the activity of the sea have played an important part in shaping the county's coastline. Undoubtedly, those processes have also played an significant part in shaping the county's islands.

The changing nature of the Essex coastline is something which might bear further study. Much has been written in recent years about the rise in sea level in the south east as a result of global warming, something which has been going on at one speed or another since Roman times.

With any significant rise in sea level not only would many of our present day islands disappear, but hillocks of land on what is now coastal mainland would themselves become Essex islands. The very earliest cases of flooding were probably just as bad in terms of physical inundation as those in recent centuries (the first recorded flooding in Essex was as long ago as 31 A.D., so the destruction of land by floodwaters is not new), but the loss of life was never so great as in recent times because island occupation was considerably less.

Hilda Grieve recorded in her 1959 publication *The Great Tide* (of which more later) that the close links between Essex and the sea were emphasised by the fact that, although the county was then some 1,528 square miles in size, nowhere was it more than about 34 miles from tidal water. Despite subsequent administrative reorganisations the figures today must still be of about the same order, though the 300 miles of seawall which stretched around the Essex coastline in the 1950s has almost certainly increased since then.

The course I propose to take on the ensuing journey around the Essex islands is a geographical one, starting in the south with the Canvey Group and working north through the Essex Archipelago, the Crouch & Blackwater Group and the Mersea Group to the Walton Backwaters & the River Stour. This is done partly for the sake of making the subject more accessible to the general reader and partly because it will allow an understanding of the various roles that Fate has set down for each island over the centuries as a consequence of its location. Virtually all of the county's islands are to be found in rivers or river estuaries and the different natures of the rivers involved and the uses to which Mankind has put them cannot help but to have rubbed off on the islands with whose care they have been entrusted. The River Thames, in particular, has always been the major route in south-eastern England for trade, recreation and invasion and various reminders of these activities can be traced through the centuries to the landscape features of the present day.

A geographical approach need not, of course, imply that, for example, all the islands in the River Blackwater share the same characteristics, or that an island in the Walton Backwaters will not have anything in common with one in Vange Creek - that this is untrue will itself become apparent as the journey unfolds - but it is certainly fair to assert that, to some degree or other, the historical, cultural and social development of each individual island has in some way been shaped by its geographical location.

The three largest Essex islands - Canvey, Foulness and Mersea - all have well-established human communities and have consequently been provided with good roads connecting them to the mainland (though some of their inhabitants might dispute this!). The smaller islands, in contrast, tend either to be uninhabited or to be occupied by just one home or farmstead. The background to this is that the larger islands tended to be major stopping off points for invading armies and sea-borne tradesmen. Communities grew up there rapidly and expanded and extended as time went on.

A consequence of this disparate level of occupation is that the history of those islands which have been or still are being occupied by Mankind is without exception better documented than that of those which have never been inhabited, if only because 'History' is the concept of human association with a place and the usefulness of that place to Man. Conversely, it might also be observed that those islands about which not much is known could therefore be said to have more to offer to the true island hunter, in terms of the as yet undiscovered potential which they may possess. It is, after all, only natural that more should be recorded and more known about islands which have had importance for humans over the years than for those which have not. This book reflects that imbalance and makes no attempt to redress it.

The Essex mainland is, despite its general flatness, widely noted for its diversity, from the extensive residential and industrial areas in the south to the rural and agricultural areas in the north, and the nature of its islands is in this respect no different from the rest of the county, Indeed, the isolation offered by many of these islands has even increased their variety, as some have been the proving grounds for a whole succession of unlikely experiments. From Angora rabbit breeding, through the establishment of a home for inebriates to the development of weapons and high explosives for war - all have been put to the test on Essex islands. Even on islands which have not witnessed attempts at such incredible projects, including those which are home to thousands of human inhabitants, there are invariably vast areas of desolate uninhabited marshland where it is still possible to 'get away from it all'.

It is perhaps significant that even those who do not live on an island all year round are more than happy to take the opportunity to visit one. The Isle of Wight, the Channel Islands and the Isle of Man remain popular tourist destinations, while St Michael's Mount in Cornwall has a constant stream of visitors to its shores in the summer. The principal industries on all islands which have significant numbers of human inhabitants are either marine- or tourist-related, even if only seasonally so. In Essex, both Canvey and Mersea Islands have their own heritage museums, tourist attractions and souvenir and gift shops and, perhaps more significantly, they are places where people deliberately plan to spend a week or two of their lives. The populations of both these islands very often increase dramatically in the summer.

A visit to an Essex island can be a most rewarding experience and if all these pages do is instil in you a desire to experience some of that reward for yourself then this book will have served something of its purpose. The magical attractions of those childhood stories really are there to be explored.

Crossing point to Rushley Island

Remains of old barges, Northey Island

## THE CANVEY GROUP

The first group of islands in this tour around the county from south to north is the Canvey Group. This is a group of islands, centred on Canvey Island itself, which lies at the junction of Holehaven Creek and the River Thames and where Benfleet Creek separates Canvey from the mainland.

The most important island in the group is of course Canvey itself, but other islands covered by this chapter include the sub-group in Vange and Holehaven Creeks (Pitsea Hall Island, Fobbing Horse, Little Fobbing Horse, Upper Horse and Lower Horse), plus Two Tree Island and the largest of the smaller marshland areas between Two Tree and Canvey, Marks Horse (covered in the Canvey chapter). With the possible exception of Two Tree Island, these smaller islands are not very widely known, as many of them are tucked away in creeks out of sight of all but the yachtsman or watersports enthusiast, or the adventurous walker. Pitsea Hall Island, which abounds with recreational attractions, is perhaps an exception, although the many people who visit it may not be aware that it is an island, as it is now connected to the mainland and it is not obvious that one is driving from one to the other.

Taken together, this group of islands provides a lot of useful facilities, ranging from homes (on Canvey) and recreational facilities (Canvey, Two Tree, Pitsea Hall) to important wildlife habitats (all of them). In this built-up south-eastern corner of the county, the Canvey Group of islands offers plenty of space and plenty of interest. It is still very possible here to 'get away from it all'.

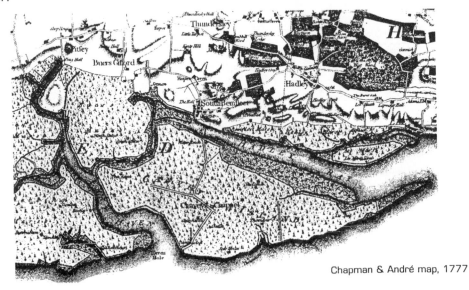

Chapman & André map, 1777

## CANVEY ISLAND

*"Whenever anyone mentions Essex, people immediately think of Canvey Island."*
Editorial in the *Basildon Evening Echo*

Where else could a journey through Essex islands begin but with Canvey, the most famous and most densely populated of all the county's islands?

Six miles long and four miles wide at its greatest extent, Canvey Island lies on the northern bank of the River Thames, in the Borough of Castle Point, halfway between Basildon and Southend-on-Sea and some 25 miles from London. It is joined to the mainland at South Benfleet by two road bridges which are barely sufficient, as many of its 35,000 residents will tell you, to cater for the constantly increasing demands of modern-day motor traffic.

Canvey's inhabitants are very proud of and protective towards their island, resisting any unwelcome intrusion from outside, much as the seawall which entirely surrounds it continues to resist the attentions of the sea. Apart from one or two minor natural undulations across the island and the modern, man-made landfill site at Newlands, the seawall is the only part of Canvey that is actually above sea-level and before the commencement of the current wall in the mid-1950s the island was regularly flooded. Indeed, the nationwide fame of Canvey is owed almost entirely to the publicity it received following the tragic flooding of the island by what came to be known as the 'Great Tide', of January and February, 1953, when 58 islanders lost their lives to the waters and many thousands more were made homeless.

The story of this inundation, which affected not just Canvey but the whole of eastern England and extensive parts of the Netherlands, has already been told admirably by Hilda Grieve in *The Great Tide*, so the details of the tragedy do not need to be repeated in full here. What it does serve to illustrate well, however, is that the occupation of any island is always at the very least a challenge and at the worst life-threatening, as the sea is constantly trying to reclaim all low-lying land, such as that at Canvey, which has been taken from it. A book on islands cannot help but make reference to this threat and in view of this an example of the magnitude provided by the flooding of Canvey serves better than any other to illustrate the often precarious nature of island life.

Canvey, of course, is not exceptional in respect of its former propensity to inundation. Every single island in Essex has suffered flooding at some time or other in its life and seawalls have progressively been raised over the years to protect each one. Before the Great Tide the most serious outcome for a flooded island was normally only the damage done to its valuable agricultural land. Even most of those islands which were occupied had only one or two people living on them, so the risk to life was not great. In 1953, when gale force winds combined with a high spring tide to bring extensive flooding to coastal areas throughout eastern England, Canvey's population was 11,500.

The statistics provided by the Great Tide itself are frightening. The flood water at its height was 20 feet deep in places. The high spring tide of the night of 31st January, whipped up by gale force winds moving southwards down the east coast, was 18 inches higher than previously recorded and the height of water in the River Thames was eight feet above predicted levels. Apart from the 58 fatalities, some 10,000 people were left homeless on Canvey. Many hundreds of animals suffered, too, including livestock, pets (more domestic animals were kept here than anywhere else in Essex that suffered flooding at the time) and countless wild animals. So many earthworms were killed that the Canvey Horticultural Society later had to 'import' some from the mainland to redress the natural balance.

The areas of the island which suffered the most from this inundation were those on the eastern side which had been reclaimed in the mid-19th century and which were known locally as Sixty Acres, Forty Acres, Sunken Marsh and Newlands. The seawalls here, lower than those fronting the Thames, soon collapsed under the weight of the floodwater. The houses, predominantly chalets and bungalows, were soon themselves under water and many were in danger of being swept away. Surviving photographs of these areas under flood bring home the horror of what it was like when the floodwaters broke.

Only the area around Canvey Village, the highest point on the island, remained relatively free from serious flooding and it was here, at the *Red Cow* public house, renamed the *King Canute* in memory of the part the hostelry played in the disaster, that the Headquarters for the flood relief operations was established. Apart from anything else, over half a million sandbags were filled on the inn's forecourt during the ensuing rescue operations. Understandably, it was many, many weeks before island life could revert to anything like its normal state.

In 1997 a campaign by a local man, Vincent Heatherson, to provide a memorial for those who died in the tragedy culminated in the dedication of a plaque outside Canvey Library. The unveiling ceremony took place on Saturday, 1st February, 1997 - 44 years to the day after the event - and was well-attended by Canvey people. Although particularly horrific, the flooding caused by the Great Tide was merely the worst in a long line of flood disasters for Canvey, though the subsequent strengthening and raising of the seawalls all round by as much as three feet and the damming of Tewkes and Smallgains Creeks, major chinks in the armour of the island's eastern defences, should ensure that a disaster of the magnitude of 1953 is never repeated.

Yet the story of Canvey begins long before 1953 - the island was already developed as an important settlement site as early as Roman times. At least four separate settlements from this period have been identified, each probably representing a small farmstead. A Roman cemetery has also been located off the eastern end of the island and a wide range of pottery vessels has been successfully extracted from it.

The presence of so many graves and the discovery of some particularly rich items of pottery and glassware, coupled with evidence that the island was the centre of a large local salt-making industry (demonstrated by the existence of some coloured mounds known as 'Red Hills'), has been said to indicate that a prosperous community once existed on the island, probably some time between 50 and 250 A.D.. The Romans may even have used Canvey as a port, as there is some evidence that ships carrying cargoes to London unloaded some of their wares on the island, apparently for distribution to adjacent mainland areas of south-east Essex. A Roman road may well have existed to facilitate this distribution, leading first to Chelmsford and then on to the important strategic Roman settlement at Colchester.

Certainly the island's geographical position, on the edge of the River Thames, itself a gateway to London and for centuries a major route for trade, leisure and invasion, has made it an almost inevitable stopping-off point for tradesmen and invading armies alike, so it is not surprising that the Romans discovered and settled Canvey, albeit in relatively small numbers. A later more famous visitor, the *Mayflower*, is also said to have stopped here to pick up pilgrims and provisions in the prelude to its momentous, history-making journey to the New World in 1620.

There is some evidence that Canvey was occupied before the Romans came, perhaps in the first few decades A.D., as fragments of early Celtic 'gritted ware' pottery have been found there. It is unlikely, however, that the nature of this occupation was anything other than domestic, as the small number of finds would appear to rule out any kind of industrial occupation. Neolithic axes, a Bronze Age bracelet and early Iron Age pottery are amongst other important archæological discoveries unearthed on the island.

Some historians have claimed that Canvey is shown on one of the oldest known maps, that of the Alexandrian geographer, Claudius Ptolemaeus Ptolemy, which was prepared in 100 A.D., as an island called 'Counos' (or 'Covennos') which, under some interpretations, is positioned in the Thames where Canvey is to be found today. Recent research, however, seems to suggest that this is not, in fact, the case, as the location of Counos on Ptolemy's map is directly over the mouth of the River Thames and not as far down into the river as modern-day Canvey. Although the landscape is certain to have changed to some extent over the intervening centuries (the island could be as much as 13 feet lower today than it was in the first century A.D.), it seems unlikely that it would have changed so radically as to enable a raised area of land to progress several miles westward up the Thames.

Additional evidence which helps to discount the suggestion that Canvey is Counos is further provided by the authority on place names, Dr P. H. Reaney, who suggests that the name 'Canvey' is derived from the Anglo-Saxon Caningaege - the "island of Cana's people" - (much later than Ptolemy) which might well have become 'Caneweye' and, "with the same confusion of 'w' and 'v' as in other places", the later 'Caneveye'.

Indeed, geological evidence seems to suggest that Canvey may well have been part of the mainland in the first century, becoming an island, or even a number of islands, as a result of land submergence in mid-Roman times. Counos itself is most likely now to be an area of land which has been demoted from an island to a mere sandbank.

Whatever the truth of the matter, the actual use of the island was changing all the time, so much so that by Anglo-Saxon times the Romans' chief occupations of salt-making and pottery manufacture had given way to farming and the island was predominantly being used for the grazing of sheep, notably those of the 'fat-tailed' variety. The alluvial nature of the soil made pasture here very rich and valuable, qualities shared with most other Essex islands and coastal areas, though continued flooding at high tide made permanent inhabitation both impractical and undesirable. The only human occupants at this time were the shepherds who looked after the sheep and these naturally tended to remain on the few areas of high ground that were available.

Huge cheeses were made from the sheep's milk to supplement the islanders' meagre income and these were sold to ships calling in to stock up with provisions on their way down the Thames.

Sheds, called 'wicks', were specially erected for the manufacture of these cheeses and modern names such as Northwick, Furtherwick and Knightswick owe their origins to this period. This cheese-making process actually became so important that in later centuries cheese was taken in large quantities to

London markets and at one stage it was even exported through Calais to the continent.

In the ninth century came the Danes, who may well have built a fortress here to store the goods which they had plundered from other areas. They were certainly here c. 893 at the Battle of Benfleet, when Danish ships in Benfleet Creek, under the command of Haesten, their king (there are various spellings of his name), were destroyed by King Alfred's son, Edward, and their invading army forced to retreat. Haesten's wife and sons were captured in the battle which took place within sight of Canvey and the surviving ships were taken to London and Rochester for use by English seamen. Charred relics and human remains dating from this period were found on the mainland at Benfleet in the 19th century, when the new railway station there was being constructed.

Mediæval times saw much change taking place on the island. The confiscation of land by King Henry II led to the redistribution of areas of Canvey into the ownership of a wide spread of important individuals. This process of redistribution was ultimately the reason for the island's early administrative structure, under the disjointed control of nine local parishes (Bowers Gifford, Hadleigh, Laindon, Leigh-on-Sea, North and South Benfleet, Pitsea, Prittlewell, Southchurch and Vange) and was to cause many arguments and administrative difficulties in later years.

But things were not all bad and the first steps were also taken at this time to protect Canvey from the constant attentions of the tides, which had continually been an obstacle to permanent human habitation, by the erection of a complete and brand new encircling seawall.

Sir Henry Appleton, the island's chief landowner, signed an agreement with Dutchman Joas Croppenburg in 1622 for the reclamation of land and the construction of a wall which would completely encircle the island. Previous sea defences had been attempted and small numbers of settlers were gradually creeping on to the island along with the shepherds and their animals, but the area was still generally very unhealthy and flooding was a regular occurrence. Women and children particularly were rare permanent inhabitants.

By this stage, cattle were as much a part of island life as the sheep were, their milk being added to that of the latter to make the cheeses more palatable, and the need for the retention of unspoilt pasture to sustain these animals was therefore correspondingly increasing. The Dutch had already proved their competence in the art of seawall construction by erecting sea defences in Lincolnshire and Dagenham in Essex and Croppenburg drew many of his own ideas from his native Holland, where numerous successful schemes had already

Dutch Cottage Museum, Canvey Island

Canvey Island Heritage Museum, formerly St Katherine's church

been introduced to combat the threat of encroachment by the sea against equally low-lying areas of land.

There is some speculation that Cornelius Vermuyden, a relative of Croppenburg's and a pupil of another notable land reclamation expert, Jacob Van Kamper, who was supervising repairs to the seawall at Dagenham, was also involved in the operation, but there is no indisputable proof to substantiate this claim (though one of the island's schools now bears his name!).

What is known, is that some 300 Dutchmen were involved in the project, which successfully enclosed some 3,600 acres. A third of this was handed over to the workers as payment for their efforts and many stayed on after the work had been completed to farm the land they had reclaimed. The original wall was built of chalk, clay and sandy limestone and was faced with Kentish ragstone which had probably been brought across the Thames from quarries near Maidstone. Dykes were cut to take the surface water from the fields and sluices were provided through the wall to discharge any excess of rainwater into the sea. All in all, the operation was a great success.

Two cottages belonging to the Dutch remain from this time - one by Northwick Corner and the other at the junction of Canvey Road and Haven Road, dated ´1618 and 1621 respectively. The former is now a museum, officially opened in 1962 by Mr. Van Ekelen from the Dutch Embassy in London following a donation to Canvey Council. It was at one time a labourer's cottage for nearby Hill Hall Farm, which had been built two years earlier in 1616 and which was demolished in 1932. Later it became a school where sewing, sums and reading were taught at a cost of fourpence a week. At least one of the school's pupils came from Benfleet. Subsequently a residence and a popular tea rooms, it has also seen use as a weekend holiday home for a city physician. Both surviving cottages were built with brick foundations and solid mud walls, kept in place by a pargetting of cockle shells, and both were originally thatched. A third surviving cottage was blown down by a gale early in the 20th century.

The distinctive octagonal design of these cottages was said to serve two purposes. Firstly, it was thought that the weight of the building could be more easily supported on what was predominantly marshy ground if it had eight points of contact with the soil instead of the more conventional four. Secondly, the overtly superstitious Dutch workers considered that, as the buildings had no corners, there was nowhere in the cottages where the Devil could hide! Even so, the Dutch have not entirely escaped association with the supernatural on Canvey. It has been reported several times that the ghost of a Dutchman has been seen on the island, dressed in appropriate 17th century attire and usually heading in the direction of the *Oysterfleet* public house!

Once the Dutch seawall was complete and a comparatively healthy atmosphere had been generated, more and more local people began to move onto the island to share the newly-reclaimed land with their foreign counter-parts. Unfortunately, however, there was some initial animosity between the two communities, generated largely by differing agricultural methods and arguments over who was responsible for seawall repairs. These acrimonious exchanges reached a particular height when the Dutch were granted special permission to erect a chapel on the island and to have church services in Dutch in the building, whilst English churchgoers were not allowed to use the chapel and were forced to continue to worship at St Mary's church in South Benfleet on the mainland.

By 1665, when England was at war with Holland, the friction between the two communities was at its height. Two years later, part of the attacking Dutch fleet made a memorable trip up the Thames towards London and, after destroying the tower of East Tilbury church further upstream, returned to Canvey where they anchored in Holehaven Creek and made a raid on the island, taking sheep and provisions and burning down farms, houses and barns as they did so. The raid was organised by Admiral Van Ghent against the orders of the more senior Admiral Michiel de Ruyter and the former was later punished for his actions. Contemporary accounts tell of the burning of one house and the destruction of eight others, the burning of barns, the theft of small boats and a catalogue of other thefts and misdemeanours. The belief that the Admiral had been invited to raid the island by Dutchmen already resident there was soon widely circulated and it was not too long before many of the Dutch settlers who had stayed on the island after their work on the seawalls was completed had moved on to pastures new, leaving behind them only the fruits of their labours and their quaint little cottages.

For everyone left on the island it was not just Dutch raiders who were a problem. The creation of new land from the sea had been almost haphazard and disputes over ownership and the responsibility of individual landholders to maintain the seawalls soon became increasingly frequent and ill-tempered. As the years dragged on and the disputes continued, the seawalls began to be neglected and many soon fell into disrepair.

The system was supposed to work as follows: any land enclosed after the Dutch seawall was built was called Outsands and it was the responsibility of its owners to maintain it individually as best they could. Lands inside the wall were called Freelands or Third Acre Lands, depending on whether they were already in existence before the Dutch came or whether they had been reclaimed from the sea during the seawall construction. As only the owners of the Third Acre Lands, who were generally the Dutch settlers, were liable to pay rates towards the upkeep of the seawall there was a considerable amount of argument between neighbouring landowners. The entire system was costly, ineffective and difficult to administer and the walls tended to be neglected as a result. By 1736, when the whole of the south-east suffered from severe storm and flood damage, the island was under water again.

In 1792 an Act of Parliament was introduced to set up a body known as the Commissioners of Sewers for Canvey Island which was authorised to levy fees on Freelands landholders for the raising of funds to rebuild the seawall where necessary if it was not possible to pay for adequate repairs using money contributed by only the Third Acre landowners. The first meeting of this body was held at the *Anchor* in South Benfleet and, although by all accounts not entirely satisfactory, it did go some way to improving the system for ensuring that repairs to the island's seawalls were carried out as and when the occasion demanded.

The numbers of people living on Canvey continued to increase and by Victorian times there was much residential development of the island by wealthy landowners taking place. This in turn led to a corresponding improvement in the everyday way of life there. New areas of land were reclaimed (it was these which suffered most in 1953) and seven 250-feet deep artesian wells were sunk to provide the growing population with a long-overdue and much-needed supply of fresh water.

In 1872 the Reverend Henry Hayes came to Canvey as its first full-time minister of the Church of England and he worked hard to develop community life on the island. Over the next few years Reverend Hayes introduced a number of significant changes to island life. He re-sited the church which had by now replaced the humble Dutch chapel some 20 feet further back into the churchyard and substantially enlarged it, giving it a new dedication to St Katherine (now the island's Heritage Centre). He also built a vicarage, sunk a well and established a school on the island and was almost single-handedly responsible for the development of the area around the *Red Cow* (*King Canute*), known today as Canvey Village.

In 1881 Canvey became a parish in its own right. This development gave islanders more freedom of choice and a major say in planning their futures, but it could not guarantee them a life without problems. The nationwide agricultural depression was then at its height and arable farming, which had long since replaced pasture as the principal type of land usage on the island, was one of those areas that was particularly badly hit. Employment on Canvey at this time was still almost exclusively in agriculture and, amongst other business sidelines, there was a thriving 'export' trade in hay, much of which is said to have been bound for the stables of many horse-racing Derby winners. Some farms even had their own wharves constructed to facilitate the loading of the commodity on to London-bound barges.

But agricultural depression was not the only disaster that lay in store for Canvey. In that same year a fierce gale and surging tides led to yet another collapse in the seawalls and the island flooded all over again. Some 1200 acres were submerged on this occasion, with three miles of seawall on the eastern side of the island being severely damaged. In some places the top of the wall was carried away completely and the whole island was in danger of being flooded with the coming of the next tide. Five hundred men, including 150 soldiers ferried across the Thames from their base at Chatham in Kent, worked desperately all day to repair the breaches, which were particularly severe between Scarhouse and Leigh Beck. Equipment, materials and men all had to wait for a suitable tide to be ferried across the creek from their rendezvous point at Benfleet railway station.

Although the island had been flooded countless times before and many steps had been taken over the years in an attempt to provide inhabitants with adequate anti-flood protection, there is no doubt that the 1881 flooding marked a turning point in Canvey's sea defence history. The Third Acre landowners, still primarily responsible for financing the maintenance of adequate sea defences, could not, on this occasion, provide enough money to pay for the necessary repairs. Of particular annoyance to the Third Acre owners was the fact that it was the privately maintained defences of many of the comparatively newly-reclaimed Outsands lands which were invariably the most likely to give way. The inadequate provisions of the 1792 Act were quickly replaced by new legislative measures. The Canvey Island (Sea Defences) Act of 1883 radically altered the responsibilities for wall maintenance and gave the Commissioners even more powers to ensure that sufficient repair work was promptly carried out. Under this new legislation, all the island's occupants became liable to contribute towards the upkeep of its defences once the Third Acre rate exceeded a statutory minimum amount. The walls of the Outsands were also brought under the control of the Commissioners, who immediately instituted a programme of raising all walls on the island to a height of at least 12 inches above the highest recorded tides (up to two feet on areas fronting the River

Thames). This virtually voided the 1622 Anglo-Dutch agreement and gave island inhabitants generally considerably more peace of mind.

But the sea knows nothing of statutes and in spite of these radical improvements the island was to suffer yet another inundation even before the century was out. On 29th November, 1897 (known at the time as 'Black Monday'), the county was hit by another strong gale. The roof of the ancient *Lobster Smack* public house was blown off and many stretches of the seawall cracked and broke under the combined pressure of wind and wave action. Not for the first or last time on Canvey, northerly gales coincided with a high spring tide and the island, along with most of the Essex coastline, was flooded again. In fact, virtually all of the county's islands, except for the central part of the rather higher-lying Mersea Island, were affected to a greater or lesser degree by the Black Monday floods. Fortunately no deaths were recorded, largely because the storm had struck at midday and people could see the situation as it unfolded before their eyes and take steps to avoid it. The floodwaters, however, remained on the island for four weeks, something which caused extensive long-term damage to the land.

Subsequent remedial works were to be successful in keeping Canvey flood-free for half a century, but many of those who experienced the flooding at the time found it almost impossible to have any confidence in their future there. Crops were still poor in many parts of the island until 1899 and many landholders, incensed at the increased seawall charges which had to be levied to finance yet more repairs to the badly damaged seawalls and disillusioned by the poor state of agriculture and the prospect of further depression brought about by the flood, began to sell their property and move out. Perhaps not surprisingly, because of the traditional financial burden which they had had to bear, many of the Third Acre lands failed to sell and a comparative study of the distribution of those lands with the built-up areas of modern Canvey reveals that it is mostly the Third Acre lands which have been left undeveloped. The problems caused by Third Acre land classification would not be completely removed until the introduction of yet another new Act in 1933.

A guidebook of the island from this time describes Canvey as "a wild and forbidding place... of somewhat repulsive aspect", with a "peculiar population", a coastguards' hamlet close to the seawall by the *Lobster Smack* and several separate "villages" (known as Canvey, Knightswick, Panhole and Lovis). "There," the guidebook continues, "is a scant population of people who have their own ways, their own traditions and their own methods of regarding a stranger. They are singularly hospitable and the people expect and give kindness. On a gusty night, when the rushes moan and shiver, and the great river sounds hoarsely, it is hardly possible to look out into the darkness without feeling a sense of strangeness and even of fear. It is better to seek the hospitable shelter of an inn, and put up with rough fare, or any fare, rather than remain in the open amid that abomination of desolation."

The most obvious place to find shelter at this time would probably have been the *Lobster Smack* inn, perhaps the most famous building on Canvey and almost certainly the oldest - parts of it appearing to date from the 16th century. It was formerly known as the *World's End* and is said to be the model for the Sluice House in Charles Dickens' *Great Expectations* (Sluice House Farm once stood nearby).

Before the new sea defences were erected the inn was perched precariously on the very edge of the island, close to the point where the deep waters of Holehaven Creek offered shelter for vessels as a stopping-off point. Now it is dwarfed by the modern concrete and steel defences of the 1970s and 1980s, but remains an extremely popular public house and meeting place.

During the 1800s a large number of illegal bare-knuckle prize fights were staged outside the inn, which was remote enough in its isolated spot by the river for the sport's participants not to have to worry about being troubled by the law. The inn itself was used as the changing quarters for the fights, which were publicised solely by word-of-mouth. Even so, a large crowd was often present to witness the activities of fighters such as Nat Langham, Ben Caunt and Tom Sayers, known to many as "the greatest champion of them all". These fights were punishing affairs and could last anything up to 85 rounds until a victory was recorded.

In January, 1857, a particularly memorable contest was fought at the inn between Sayers and Aaron Jones. After an incredible 65 rounds it ended as a draw only because the light was fading as dusk approached. Five years later, across the river at Fobbing, the two top combatants, Jem Mace and Tom King, met for one of the most eagerly awaited fights in English boxing history. King won and received a prize of £300 for his efforts.

As well as being the scene of prizefighting, the *Lobster Smack* also played host for many years to an annual fair where a variety of goods such as toys, ribbons, gingerbread and fruit were sold. The fair took place on 25th June each year and was in full swing as early as 1767. It was still a regular feature of island life in 1848, but by 1889 it had disappeared for good.

Like many other coastal areas, Canvey had a long tradition of smuggling throughout the 17th and 18th centuries and the *Lobster Smack* was a popular haunt of the island's smugglers. Tales have been told of smugglers' lights flashing signals at night from the ruined tower of nearby Hadleigh Castle on the mainland to ships lying out in the river and of contraband being stashed in houses hereabouts. Coastguard cottages and a look-out tower were built near the hostelry in a vain attempt to combat some of this activity. These cottages still stand and were recently restored, though in September, 1999, they were badly damaged by fire.

Strange as it may seem, however, with such a background as this, Canvey was, at the end of the 19th century, on the verge of a remarkable transformation. Things which happened at this time were to set the scene for much of the island's development throughout the next hundred years.

Much of the land which sold at the time of the Black Monday floods was purchased by an enthusiastic and far-sighted entrepreneur named Frederick Hester, who, in 1899, acquired Leigh Beck Farm and began work on a residential scheme for the construction of bungalows, which he called the 'Southview Park Estate'. The speed with which Hester's first few properties sold encouraged him to buy up more plots of land and to build more bungalows. He had initially planned them as places where city people would spend their summer holidays and week-ends, but the scheme progressed so well that he was soon deliberately marketing them as 'dream homes' for London's East-enders to whom the attractions of a cheap rural seaside lifestyle were far preferable to the squalor of the City.

Hester had great ambitions for the development of Canvey as a seaside resort for Londoners. Attractions he provided to entice them included a promenade and a pier on the river front (the latter later being extended by the incorporation of some solidified cement barrels rescued from a convenient shipwreck which took place off the coast in 1902) and a magnificent Winter Garden and Palace, a project of semi-tropical glasshouses which was planned to cover six square miles and to include a 'Venetian canal' which would link up with the natural lake which can still be seen on the island. (This lake, originally part of Small Gains Creek, was used by the Romans as an oyster bed. It was dammed off by Dutch engineers when they reclaimed the island and is now an interesting nature conservation area.) Hester marketed his properties ruthlessly, advertising Canvey as 'Ye Olde Dutch Island' and giving many of his newly created roads Dutch-sounding names. A monorail (initially horse-drawn, later electric), carried passengers around the island, its attendants being attired in traditional Dutch costume. Free rail tickets were offered to potential purchasers from London, refreshments were laid on and, at Christmas, turkeys were given away to those who were actually keen enough to part with their money. A later aspect of the scheme included a proposed tramway extension across the head of the Hadleigh Ray to Leigh-on-Sea to join the existing tramway network of Southend, but this plan (a forerunner of latter day proposals to build a road across the creek there) never saw the light of day.

Hester had not been the first to see the prospect for tourism on the island. In the mid-1880s Canvey's attractions as a holiday resort had been publicised in a booklet entitled *New Holidays in Essex*, with supporting illustrations of a Dutch cottage and the *Lobster Smack* inn. His success, however, far surpassed that of any previous entrepreneur, largely as a result of his energetic and innovative publicity methods, which included setting up an estate office on platform four at Fenchurch Street station where land was sold by auction every Wednesday and Thursday. The success of Hester's campaigns introduced the name of Canvey to thousands of non-locals for the first time in its history.

In 1901 over a thousand plots of land were set aside for building on Hester's Southview Park Estate, a move which signalled the start of a period of intensive development on the island. Three years later a land auction held over the Whitsun bank holiday attracted sales worth £600. By this stage a large wooden tower topped by a specimen bungalow had been erected by Hester to enable prospective purchasers to see both a show home and the whole island at the same time. A mile of the Winter Gardens glasshouse scheme had also been constructed, as had 400 feet of pier.

The horse-drawn monorail was about to be replaced by an electric railway and, by summer, 4,000 railway sleepers had been unloaded in preparation for the work ahead. Four 25-seater carriages, in red and gold and with the words "Venice-on-Sea and Canvey" painted on the side, were also delivered. Things were going extremely well. In July alone, 2,000 people visited Canvey and £1,000 worth of land was sold. Throughout the autumn work progressed well and the railway was being used to transport materials around the island.

By November, however, delays in the delivery of materials began to give Hester great problems and when one person refused to allow the tramway to go across his land, the scheme fell into a rapid decline. By April, 1905, it was beyond salvation. The tramway's materials were sold off by auction at Chimney's Farm, Hester became bankrupt and the project folded. This incredible scheme had lasted barely five years.

Despite his bankruptcy, Hester had set in motion developments which would ultimately see Canvey being transformed into the Londoners' resort which he had always envisaged. The focus of population was already moving away from

Canvey Village, which Reverend Hayes had been instrumental in developing, to areas at the eastern end of the island around Small Gains and Leigh Beck which Hester had originally bought from many of the departing farmers. As Hester had always intended Canvey to be a healthy resort he had introduced certain conditions of sale to any land which he passed on to ensure that there was to be no industrial development of land which had at any time been in his ownership. The wide publicity which the island had received, however, attracted the attentions of businessmen as well as those of simple home-owners and the cheap land which was readily available there led to a sudden influx of industrial proposals, many of which were based around the natural deep water facilities at Hole Haven.

Despite the increasing outside attention, island life was still fairly primitive. The only way on to Canvey was across the creek by boat when the tide was in or on foot by conveniently placed stepping stones when the tide was out. Some actually tried to drive carts across at low tide, but the mud claimed many victims who could not maintain sufficient momentum to clear the creek and reach the other side. As the population grew, the problems of providing adequate freshwater and sewerage facilities became increasingly acute. Deep water wells were bored in several places and a pumping station was introduced, but it was well into the 1950s before the situation was resolved to everybody's satisfaction.

But things were not all bad. Drainage was improved and the seawalls were being maintained in a better state than they had ever been maintained before. The climate on the island was rapidly improving and the traditional unhealthy nature of island life was being eroded all the time. A livestock fair was introduced and the population continued to increase. In 1901 there were 300 people on the island; just 30 years later there were well over 3,000. Of course, some things were still slow to develop. In 1911, for example, the island had just one policeman and shared its only doctor with neighbouring Benfleet.

An advertisement for Canvey Regatta, dated 1st August, 1908, described the island as "Holland-in-England... a unique health resort. Beautiful shell beach. Good bathing. Boating and fishing. A capital harbour for yachts at Hole Haven. The far end of the island confronts the German Ocean [North Sea], commanding a fine view of the shipping continually passing. Old Dutch farms and cottages. An ancient well with thatched roof stands in the centre of the village." There was no doubt that the island had many attractions.

After the First World War, during which a number of Londoners were removed to the island in case of attacks on the Capital, another scheme was put forward for a deep water berth and goods jetty at Hole Haven, a scheme which incorporated the attractive idea of a rail connection with the mainland. The idea was turned down, but an interest in industrial development on Canvey had been rekindled and, in the longer term, industrial use would be the eventual outcome for many parts of the island, particularly the southern and south-western areas facing the Thames.

Canvey at this time was still proving very popular with day-trippers and casual visitors. At Easter in 1924 wonderful sunshine attracted record crowds, whilst in August some 15,000 people visited the island. Two years later an incredible 50,000 people turned out for the August bank holiday, many of them waiting an hour for a boat to become available to take them across Benfleet Creek from the mainland. Long-stay visitors were also being wooed: a booklet from this time claimed that "a week in Canvey will do you more good than a fortnight elsewhere".

In 1926 Canvey's population had grown to such an extent that the island was able to achieve Urban District Council status. One of the new Council's first actions was to refuse another planning application for an industrial development at Hole Haven (at Brickhouse Farm), which was done on the grounds that it would damage the status of Canvey as a resort. This, however, only amounted to a postponement of the inevitable - the case eventually went to the House of Lords and the Council's decision was overturned. The land involved was taken over by London & Coastal Oil Wharves, who acquired a long lease on the estate.

At about this time (in 1931), plans were put forward for a bridge across Benfleet Creek to link Canvey by road to the mainland. The existing 'road' leading to the island, which had been laid down next to the original stepping stones to provide for both horse & cart and the increasingly popular motor vehicle, was only passable at low tide and this was proving to be quite impractical.

The original plan for a high-level bridge costing £150,000 was beyond the Council's budget so a cheaper alternative, in the form of an opening roller-bridge powered by electric motors, was introduced. Designed by London architect, Gerald Dean, it cost just £20,000. The opening of this bridge was such a momentous event for islanders that a special one-day 'public holiday' was declared.

The improved access that the bridge provided and the precedent set by the London & Coastal oil development ultimately led to more attention for the island and the floating of more industrial schemes. Canvey was near to London, cheap to develop and easily accessible. From the late 1930s onwards, industry and commercialisation began to grow side-by-side with residential inhabitation. Shops also began to spring up on many of the main roads, particularly in the High Street, which was originally literally much higher than buildings along it as it had once been part of the old Dutch seawall. Roads, lighting and beaches were all significantly improved. Residential growth became particularly evident in Canvey Village, Long Road, Furtherwick Road and at a new 'Dutch Village' off Canvey Road. Canvey Casino was opened in the mid-1930s as the first building on what is now Eastern Esplanade, pleasure boat trips to the popular Chapman lighthouse were thriving and a booklet publicising caravan and camping holidays was published. By the summer of 1938 there were over 4,000 buildings on the island.

With the coming of the Second World War Canvey found itself at the forefront of many German air raids. The island occupied a significant geographical location - on a direct route up the Thames to London - and its valuable oil installations, always distinctive and difficult to camouflage, were prime targets for bombing raids. In particular, many devices were dropped on the island during the Battle of Britain in the summer of 1940.

As a result of all this activity, two small gun forts were installed on Canvey to give it protection against air and sea attacks. At Scar's Elbow Point a twin six-pounder gun and five searchlights were set up to counteract the threat of German U-boats, whilst at Dead Man's Point (so called because of a sub-marine shelf under which victims of drowning are trapped) a battery brought into operation in the Great War was reopened. Concrete pits there contained two six-inch breech loading guns, together with a magazine and storehouses. Traces of these installations remain.

A special 1¾ mile long wooden boom was also built off the island, stretching across to St Mary's Bay on the Kent side of the river. It was equipped with three powerful searchlights, reached by a narrow-gauge railway, and had a movable middle section which could be used to block or unblock the river. Additional searchlights, torpedo tubes and a gun emplacement were set up on the island to defend the boom, along with two observation towers - one at Hole Haven and one at Coalhouse Fort further upstream. The torpedoes were actually fired on one occasion in a successful attempt to prevent a major explosion when a burning, out-of-control vessel was about to collide with the jetty on which the filled tubes were mounted. The bridge to Benfleet was deliberately booby-trapped so that it could be exploded if the Germans invaded, though this would have effectively cut the island off from the outside world, while nearby Benfleet Downs, which offered an invaluable vantage point, were laced with defensive trenches and mounted with searchlights and guns. Movement on the island was restricted and a fire station and two sub-stations were set up there. The local police force was also bolstered by the introduction of a number of civilian special constables.

The *Lobster Smack* was used in the national interest - as a shore station for the River Emergency Service (RES) under the guidance of the Port of London Authority (PLA). A number of similar stations were set up on both sides of the Thames, from Canvey to Tower Pier in London. The *Lobster Smack*, designated as "Holehaven" station, was the most seaward station on the river and its military occupants controlled the stretch of the Thames from Sea Reach to the North Sea. The inn was referred to as a 'stone frigate', the naval term for a shore establishment. In 1940 the Navy took over operations from the PLA and the upper part of the inn was converted into a mess deck, complete with beds and cooking facilities. The oil refineries hereabouts attracted much enemy attention and the inn was retained for defence purposes for a year after the war. A fire at the refineries caused by enemy bombing could take up to three weeks to put out.

The principal job of the RES was to police the river, usually with the help of commandeered crews in commandeered boats, and to advise the authorities of any suspicious movements on it.

Service personnel were equipped with machine guns and mine-marking equipment and much of their work was carried out under the cover of darkness. Specially trained Sea Scouts were also employed to log all shipping activity - the river was home to important docks at Tilbury and in East London.

It was nearly 300 years since Canvey had been in the front line of an enemy attack and the bombs and rockets which landed there were rather more advanced than the 17th century Dutch cannonballs had been. Many projectiles landed on the island throughout the war, ironically following many Londoners who had moved to Canvey to escape the dangers of the Capital.

Canvey was a different place in the 1940s from what it had been some 25 years earlier. James Wentworth Day recalled in *Coastal Adventure* how different his experiences of wartime visits there had been. "I have contrasting memories of Canvey in the two World Wars. In 1914 it was an open land of farms and marshes where, on lonely outpost duty, a man could walk all day and shoot as many partridges, hares and wild duck as a strong boy could carry." By 1945 there were very few places in the developed areas for animals like these to hide.

When it was all over, much rebuilding was required, not least because the population had dramatically increased over the war years and new facilities and services were required to support it. Many of those who had spent the period on the island stayed on when the war was over, preferring mildly bombed rural Essex to badly bombed urban London. Restrictions, however, remained in force for some time and the rebuilding of island life was a long drawn-out affair.

During this new period of development amusement arcades and other holiday resort entertainment facilities were introduced along Eastern Esplanade next to the Casino and the first holiday camp, at Thorney Bay, was established.

Over 50 islanders (from a population of what was at this stage a little over 10,000) were killed in the War. By one of Life's cruel ironies the Memorial Hall which was erected in dedication to their memory was officially opened eight years later on the night of 31st January, 1953, just hours before the arrival of the Great Tide and the deaths of a further 58 inhabitants. The war and the waters had dealt a double blow to Canvey and there were calls by many at the time to abandon occupation of the island altogether and to let the land be returned to the sea for good. But the courage and commitment of the people there, commemorated in a famous speech in which they were described as "never so great as in adversity", meant that such thoughts were never even entertained on Canvey. The island's MP, Bernard Braine (later Lord Braine of Wheatley), told other MPs at the time that Canvey would rise again, and rise it did. Island life builds strong character and community spirit. Despite the setbacks, no war and no inundation was ever going to take Canvey.

As the effects of war receded and still more and more people began to move on to the island, a need for some structured form of residential development was identified. Up until now, islanders had been left to their own, rather haphazard, devices. Kenneth Strugnell, in his book *Seagates to the Saxon Shore*, pointedly observes that at this stage "the era of the planners had not yet dawned, so that it argues a certain ingenuity on the part of the settlers that they could create such a degree of hideousness without any official assistance". But as post-war restrictions meant that very little private building land was now available to the individual settler, the local authority began to take an active part in physically shaping the island's future. The first Council houses were introduced in 1947 and the adoption of a generous lending policy and the establishment of a number of highly successful housing schemes immediately after the 1953 flood disaster by the Canvey Island Urban District Council were instrumental in encouraging people to stay on the island, at a time when many might have thought of leaving, despite a dramatic drop in house prices as a result of the uncertainty caused by the flooding. The development of a brand new estate off Long Road in conjunction with the Boroughs of Dagenham and Walthamstow was of particular significance, as several hundred homes were built there to cope with the substantial housing overspill from those two areas. The startling rejuvenation of the community after the devastation caused by the Great Tide has been compared with the resurgence of Germany as a world power during a similar period of regeneration after the Second World War.

In addition to its permanent inhabitants, the island was soon back playing host to casual visitors and holiday-makers once more. It was the first time since 1939 that many people had been able to get away for a break - a much needed break at that - and many of those who had visited Canvey in the 1930s stayed loyal to the island and returned in large numbers.

Renewed, if less welcome, attention was also being received from industrial entrepreneurs with ideas of their own for the island. These principally concerned plans for further gas and oil storage facilities. As far back as 1870, the Metropolis Sewage and Essex Reclamation Company, whose aim was to collect sewage from the end of the Northern Outfall Sewer and identify places for its disposal, had seen the potential in Canvey's geographical location and had earmarked the island's foreshore as a likely place for its activities. Fortunately for Canvey these plans never reached fruition but in the age of rebuilding after the Second World War the impetus behind new schemes was considerably greater.

Understandably, many of the islanders were opposed to industrial development, partly because of the inherent dangers in the substances involved and partly because of the detriment to their predominantly natural landscape and rural lifestyle. In August, 1951, when the Regent Oil Company was granted a licence to commence the island's biggest industrial development so far - a site of more than 30 acres which was to become an oil storage installation and depot - their worst fears were realised.

Since then the question of industrial development on the island has raised its head many times. Pressure groups have been formed each time that a new industrial development has been proposed. Sometimes they have won, sometimes they have not. Industry began to expand rapidly from the late 1950s onwards, once the Regent Oil case had been approved, and more and more oil storage facilities were introduced. A prototype natural gas installation was also developed at Canvey during this period and the scheme was so successful that shipments of liquid gas were soon being brought to the island from Algeria to be stored there at freezing temperatures. The discovery of natural gas in the North Sea later relieved some of this activity but the site was by now well and truly established and Canvey became the major gas installation location in the country.

Ironically, the nature of Canvey life - as a self-contained community with a rapidly increasing population - meant that the island was chosen in 1965 as the first place in the country where all domestic gas appliances were to be converted to use natural gas and for a time the settlement was therefore the most up-to-date in England.

As for the oil refineries, their dramatic increase was influenced to some extent by a major change in post-war industrial policy. The deep water berths offered by Thameside locations, close to London but not too close (just in case of accident), led to many new refineries being built along the river at this time. As well as the constructions on Canvey, three other massive sites were also set up at Coryton, Shellhaven and the Isle of Grain (in Kent).

By the dawn of the 1960s, the local authority was actively marketing the island's industrial potential. It was advertised that "industrial development is now being centred on two excellent sites, admirably positioned, and Canvey Island Urban District Council gives every assistance to industrialists". A series of Public Inquiries throughout the succeeding years led to the award of several planning permissions and giant companies like Occidental and United Refineries were soon making the most of the support that they had been given. Not all developments were successful, however - one of Occidental's projects was brought to a halt despite an alleged multi-million-pound cash outlay, whilst other land with full planning permission for a refinery was never built on.

Despite the fears of islanders for their safety, extensive reports produced in the late-1970s and early 1980s concluded that there was actually little or no danger from industry to those living on the island and that any risks there might once have were steadily decreasing. The Health and Safety Executive's (HSE) *Canvey: a second report* stated that "these risk reductions result not only from the direct improvements at the installations concerned but also from thorough analyses of certain potentially hazardous plants and processes and the actual or imminent closure of others".

Companies are now expected to carry out hazard surveys on certain proposed developments, particularly surveys of potential major hazards, to demonstrate that their facilities meet the strict design requirements which are now in place and that they can be operated and maintained safely once the facilities are in operation. Many of the principal complaints recently, in these times of high environmental awareness, have centred around the pollution of the River Thames through the spillage of toxic substances. The HSE's reports estimated that the chance of someone being killed by an accident at any one of the island's major industrial plants was 1 in 25,000, concluding that "there is little doubt that the lessons learned and the techniques honed at Canvey will be of great value elsewhere".

The situation today regarding Canvey's heavy industry appears to be more settled than it has been for many years. In 1994 London & Coastal's Hole Haven development was bought by Oikos Storage Ltd, which took over the massive 300,000m³ storage capacity partly for the receipt and reprocessing of waste oil and partly to rent out to other oil companies. A new water treatment plant has since been built there and the storage operation generally has been refurbished.

The Regent Oil operation, later taken over by Texaco, has since been closed down, while no substantial construction work was ever undertaken on any of the sites United Refineries had proposed to develop. Occidental's unused refinery to the west of the Regent Oil site was knocked down in 1996-7, leaving only the riverside jetty and a battered looking landscape behind it. In 1999 the jetty was sold to Newcastle-based Blue Lark, whilst the remainder of the site revealed an unexpected gem in the form of a rare marsh orchid found thriving there.

The gas installation was sold in 1996 to National Gas, who converted it to handle Liquid Petroleum Gas (LPG), importing propane and butane for subsequent road distribution. The site was later bought by its current owners, Calor Gas.

Canvey's relationship with light industry is equally well settled. In the west there is a large factory estate at Charfleet's, whilst the east end plays host to marine activities, such as Prout's famous boat yard. Roland and Francis Prout set many British records for canoeing throughout their careers and in the Helsinki Olympic Games in 1952 they equalled the previous Olympic-best time for the 100 metres. They later became more famous for the development of the catamaran.

The increased traffic generated by the growing residential and industrial development brought with it one somewhat overdue benefit - the improvement of the single road access on to the island and the provision of a second one. Traffic had increased so much that by 1973 a replacement high-level fixed bridge was provided across the creek at Benfleet in the vicinity of the now inadequate 1930s roller bridge, and then later on a second access route was opened up across the marshland to the west of the island from Sadler's Farm roundabout on the main-land. Up until this time, traffic using the old road bridge still had to give way to ships passing along the creek and in any case there were constant traffic jams (ships or no ships), often stretching up to three miles back along the road. The events of 1953 had introduced concerns about the need for speedy evacuation of the island should a disaster similar to the Great Tide occur again and these combined with latent fears about the outcome of any accident that might take place at any of the island's industrial sites to usher in an era of improved road communications. Corresponding improvements were made to island approach roads and the original level crossing at Benfleet railway station was replaced by an underpass.

A new roundabout at Waterside Farm became the junction point for both roads onto the island and so adopted a crucial role in Canvey's traffic system. This, in turn, has led to calls from some for a third road to be introduced as everyone leaving the island has currently to go through Waterside Farm and in an emergency the junction could become a severe bottleneck. Essex County Council runs an Emergency Planning section which meets with local people continually to review flood defence operations for the island and recent meetings have seemed to show that it is very unlikely that the whole island would ever need to be evacuated at once. Fears of flooding have been drastically reduced now that the Environment Agency operates a flood warning service - in conjunction with the Storm Tide Forecasting Service at the Meteorological Office in Bracknell - which gives early notice of any impending inundation, whilst on the island itself all new houses built since 1953 have had to be two-storey, the upper storey guaranteeing a place of relative safety against floodwaters if ever it should be needed. (There is actually a third route off the island, at the western end on to the Pitsea Marshes (signposted "RVP" - "Rendezvous Point"), but it is for emergency use only).

As well as the anti-flood preparations, the community infrastructure has also improved. A new church (built, appropriately, in modern 'Dutch' style) has replaced St Katherine's (because the latter was too small) and new primary and secondary schools have been constructed. In the north-eastern corner of the island the Newlands holiday camp, now generally known as "King's", grew up on an extensive area of reclaimed marshland and, apart from the land on which the new roundabout stood, over 200 acres of Waterside Farm was bought by the Council to provide a wide range of recreational and leisure facilities, including swimming, golf and other sports activities. The Knightswick shopping centre, built in the late 1970s, is now the focal point of Canvey shopping.

In 1974, during local government reorganisation across the country, Canvey was merged with Benfleet into a new area known as Castle Point, which

Canvey Lake

Canvey Transport Museum

stretched from Hadleigh Castle on the mainland to Canvey Point on the island. The island's own armorial bearings, which had been granted to the Council only three years earlier, were now null and void, though the motto of the island, *Ex Mare Dei Gratia* - "From the Sea by the Grace of God" - still remains as appropriate today as it ever was. By the early 1990s the status of the District of Castle Point had grown to such an extent that it was re-designated as a Borough, with its own mayor and a broader range of municipal powers.

The most significant developments in recent years have probably been the increase in house-building throughout the island, particularly in the building boom of the late-1980s, and the construction of a new retail park on some of the old Occidental land in the south-west. Many older houses have been demolished to make way for new estates, with land around Somnes Avenue and Thorney Bay showing noticeable increases in modern housing.

The retail park - featuring a supermarket and a restaurant, fed by a brand new road - was the eventual outcome of a range of proposals put forward for land use at the western end of the island on the large open spaces around Northwick Road. With no significant heavy industrial development taking place there, a proposal was put forward by Peter de Savary in the late-1980s for the creation of homes, schools, a country park and even a new railway station, to be known as Benfleet Parkway. That scheme foundered at the Public Inquiry stage.

Plans are currently afoot to create a new 10-acre cemetery in the vicinity of the Safeway development, as the current burial ground at St Katherine's has reached its natural capacity. There has also been talk of building a multi-million-pound marina, with accompanying shops and light industry in the Safeway location.

A regeneration programme was put in place for Canvey seafront in the late 1990s to take it into the new Millennium, with the area around the Labworth Café being the focus for redevelopment. The landfall site at Newlands - now probably the highest point on the island - looks set to become a country park.

Other changes have been taking place. In 1998 £250,000 was earmarked to clean up and convert Canvey Lake into a nature reserve, whilst a new Movie Starr cinema has also been introduced in recent years. The 1990s also saw the demolition of the Canvey Casino, the first building on Eastern Esplanade, which was evidently not considered of sufficiently historic value to retain.

As the 21st century dawns and new activities replace out-moded styles of entertainment, Canvey still seems a rather unlikely tourist destination, but with its holiday camps and sandy beaches, a golden few hundred yards of amusements and attractions such as the Heritage Centre, Dutch Cottage Museum (one of the smallest in the country) and the Castle Point Transport Museum (housed in the old island bus garage) it manages to retain appeal to the casual visitor and the island inhabitant alike.  The shallow waters off the island are popular with yachtsmen and windsurfers, fishermen and water-skiers and there is much marine activity off the island in the summer.  Water ski-ing in particular takes place to the north-east of the island between it and a smaller, mid-stream, marshland island called Marks Horse.  Many island activities are featured in local newspapers,.

In addition to all these man-made attractions and despite an abundance of residential and  industrial development, the island still manages to maintain close links with nature and possesses many important natural features and habitats.  The banks and ridges of shell at the Lesser Shell Banks off Canvey Point and neighbouring Two Tree Island (see later) are particularly important.

The saltmarsh at Canvey Point used to be enclosed as dry land by a seawall but the wall was breached during one of the many floods which have affected the island and the area has reverted to its original form.  These two natural features are sometimes in conflict, however, as the sensitive habitat of the saltmarsh has been destroyed in places by movement in the shellbanks.  Large flocks of birds of a number of species use the area extensively in the autumn and winter months.

The history of Canvey has been long and interesting, but what does the future hold in store?  A suggestion that an outer orbital route for the already overworked M25 motorway should cross the island and join it to Kent via a new bridge across the Thames is sure to be met with much opposition if it ever looks likely to become a reality.  Even so, many islanders would like the reassurance that a third proper access route would provide.  There is still no hospital on the island and there has never been a railway station, making commuting to London a little more difficult than things might on the face of it seem.  Essex County Council has in recent years considered a light railway link with Southend, so perhaps Hester's idea could come to fruition after all?

Despite its troubles, Canvey remains dear to the hearts of the many thousands of people to whom it has offered a home and the thousands more who have visited it as holiday-makers or as refugees from London's bombings during the War.  The community spirit which is evident wherever one travels on the island and the warm welcome which outsiders receive are clear indications that, come Hell or (perhaps what is more likely) high water, Canvey Island will never die.

## VANGE CREEK & HOLEHAVEN CREEK
(Pitsea Hall Island; Fobbing Horse; Little Fobbing Horse; Upper Horse;
Lower Horse)

"... *strange and desolate places...*"
BASILDON DISTRICT COUNCIL, *Wat Tyler Country Park*

To the immediate west of Canvey lies Holehaven Creek. This and its tributary, Vange Creek, are home to at least five other islands, all small and marshy but sufficiently important to be worthy of some attention. The furthest inland of the five is also the most important, so the journey through this chapter starts there and works downriver to the Thames.

Flood barrier, with Little Fobbing Horse in centre and Fobbing Horse background right

## PITSEA HALL ISLAND

The most important island today in the Vange Creek/Holehaven Creek vicinity is Pitsea Hall Island, a raised area of marshland between the upper end of Vange Creek and a dammed-off waterway known as Pitseahall Fleet.  The course of the creek has changed much over time - the village of Fobbing, once served by a tributary, is now left 'high and dry' and the road by the church which once led down to Fobbing harbour now leads just to fields.  Technically speaking, Pitsea Hall Island is really no longer an island at all, since the damming of the Fleet and the draining of adjacent land has led to it becoming absorbed into the surrounding marshland, but it is an area of much history and interest and its island origins can still be traced on maps and on the ground.

The name 'Pitsea Hall Island' comes from the fact that the area was part of the old Pitsea Hall estate (the hall was built c.1600) until the late 19th century.  The name was in regular use until Victorian times when map makers depicted it as a hillock surrounded by saltmarsh, protected by a seawall, but the term is now not very often heard.  Today the area is usually referred to as 'Wat Tyler Country Park' - the modern country park there being the most open and accessible part of the old island and the latest in a long line of uses to which it has been put.

The Fleet is said to have been dammed in the 17th century by Dutch settlers, perhaps connected with those on nearby Canvey Island.  In the late 19th century the whole Pitsea Hall estate - comprising pasture, arable land, woodland and saltings - was sold off and the island passed into the ownership of the British Explosives Syndicate, which used it as a site for the manufacture and storage of ammunition.  In 1913 three men were killed by an accident at the factory which also shattered windows in nearby Pitsea village.  In the 1930s-40s the island was used by the government for storage and after the Second World War it was used for industrial purposes and as a refuse tip.

In the early 1980s over 120 acres of former island was transformed by the local authority and opened as a country park.  The official opening ceremony was performed on 14th April, 1984, by Len Murray, General Secretary of the TUC, and is commemorated by a plaque on the wall of the park office.

The name 'Wat Tyler Country Park' comes from a leader of the Peasants' Revolt of 1381, which began in this area with unrest at Fobbing and neighbouring villages.  According to the wording on the plaque, it is "named as a memorial dedicated to those people of Essex and Kent who in the cause of liberty took part in the Peasants' Revolt of 1381".

Reconstructed cottages at Pitsea Hall Island

National Motorboat Museum

The park today has many attractions. It is - perhaps surprisingly - home to the National Motorboat Museum (opened in 1986), which includes several record-breaking craft and accompanying displays of motorboat equipment. Steam launches, powerboats and lifeboats are all featured, along with a collection of racing trophies and a library of books and photographs.

The park also houses a Rural Life museum, comprising reconstructed historic buildings like Holly Cottage - a c.1670 weatherboarded building which once stood in Hockley Road, Rayleigh - and Cooper's Cottage - a similar, early 1600s building, which was moved from Cooper's End, near Stansted Mountfitchet, when Stansted Airport was being constructed.

Other attractions include a miniature railway, craft shops, a café, an outdoor pursuits centre, a marina and some Second World War pillboxes which were built to guard the creek against invasion. Remnants of the old explosives factory can also be found. One of these has been converted into an amphitheatre.

Most important of all is the park's restored natural environment. There are several waymarked walks through hawthorn copses, wildflower fields and covered pathways and there are five hides from which to view the many species of water-loving birds that inhabit Pitseahall Fleet and another Vange Creek tributary, Timberman's Creek. Other creatures of interest include dragonflies and foxes, whilst saltmarsh plants can been seen all round the edges of the park. There are freshwater ponds, a wildlife garden full of scented flowers to attract butterflies and an area of cages which house several species of owl. The park has such diverse wildlife that it has been designated a Site of Special Scientific Interest (SSSI).

Outside the entrance to the park the Essex Horse & Pony Protection Society operates a sanctuary to look after disadvantaged horses and ponies. Some reminders of the island's industrial past are also evident. A civic amenity and recycling centre, an Anglian Water treatment plant and a steady stream of lorries visiting the nearby Cleanaway landfill site on the Pitsea Marshes all hark back to the local industrial activities of yesteryear.

In 1999 plans were unveiled for a new environmental centre at the park, incorporating conference, exhibition and leisure facilities and using all the latest energy-saving devices. This project is to be financed in part by the landfill tax credit scheme operating at Cleanaway's nearby site.

## FOBBING HORSE & LITTLE FOBBING HORSE

Downstream from Pitsea Hall Island another former island has been absorbed into the mainland in the shape of the so-called Fobbing Horse. Though now little more than a large deviation in the course of the creek, this was visible a hundred years ago as a distinct island, the channel separating it from the mainland having silted up in the interim. A small, associated island to the south is still evident midstream and is referred to in some sources as 'Little Fobbing Horse'.

The authority on English place names, Dr P. H. Reaney, records that the derivation of the name probably owes much to its appearance as a 'mud hill', from the Old English 'horsc' and 'hyll'. He also states that there is presumably some connection with the other lost place-names of 'Wodenham Horse' and 'Sea Horse' on Canvey Island, dating from 1563, which were referred to by the 18th century Essex historian, Philip Morant. The term 'hill' is also used of the saltings in Vange and Holehaven Creeks, described as a marsh in 1203. The description of the island as "Fobbing" Horse distinguishes it from other 'horse' islands further downstream (see below), identifying it as being the closest geographically to Fobbing marsh and village. Little Fobbing Horse is obviously the smaller of the two adjacent islands.

The use of the word 'horse' in relation to raised areas of land which are surrounded by water exists in a number of locations around the county and it has been used to describe both genuine islands and sandbanks. A long spit between Northey and Osea Islands in the River Blackwater near Maldon was for a long time known as the "Island Horse". From Great Cob Island, near the town of West Mersea on Mersea Island, projects a spit called the "North Horse", whilst another 'horse' area can be found near Wallasea Island in the so-called Essex Archipelago. (See later for more information on these islands.). There is also a Marks Horse island between Canvey Island and the mainland (see last chapter). All of these 'horses' signify a shallow patch or spit of sand lying in a tidal river or estuary. They are very often connected to the shore or only separated from it by a narrow channel.

Fobbing Horse's main claim-to-fame now, since it and its smaller neighbour are not easily accessible unless by a lengthy walk or by boat, is to be the foothold of one half of the Fobbing Barrier - a barrier across Vange Creek which can be used to prevent flooding in times of high tide or freak storm conditions.

## UPPER HORSE & LOWER HORSE

Nearer the Thames than Fobbing Horse, after Vange Creek has flowed into Holehaven Creek, are two other 'horse' islands. These are Upper Horse and Lower Horse, whose names have similar derivations to that quoted above.

The distinctions of 'upper' and 'lower' refer to their geographical positions in relation to the mouth of the creek, Lower Horse being nearer to the Thames than its companion. Both are essentially marshland islands, formerly of larger size and once almost one. Upper Horse today retains fragments of its former extent in the form of a collection of smaller 'satellite' islands, which can be seen from the mainland as individual marshland areas dotted around it.

The strategic significance of the River Thames throughout history has been well documented and in this area it is particularly notable in relation to the interest shown in Canvey Island by successive invasions of Roman, Danish and Dutch settlers. Upper Horse provides further evidence of this as it contains what are thought to be Roman earthworks, similar to those discovered on the mainland at nearby Hadleigh. These earthworks would seem to have been part of a fortified camp, about 250 feet square, for the garrisoning of some 500 men. Site excavation is really needed, however, before it can be conclusively proved that the work dates from Roman times.

Both these islands are now rather dwarfed by the surrounding industrial developments on Canvey Island and (especially) at Coryton and, like Fobbing and Little Fobbing Horses, it is only the enthusiastic local yachtsman or the adventurous walker who is ever likely to encounter them by accident.

Lower Horse, with refineries behind

Upper Horse, overlooked by Coryton Refineries

# TWO TREE ISLAND

*"...an island... of international importance..."*

ESSEX WILDLIFE TRUST, *Guide To Reserves*

To the north-east of Canvey Island, between Canvey and the mainland, lies Two Tree Island. Predominantly marshland, Two Tree is about the same size as Pitsea Hall Island and has a similar history - formerly a rubbish tip and now a popular nature and recreational area.

The island is divided into two distinct halves, separated east and west by the only road which leads across it over the bridge from the mainland at Leigh-on-Sea to the marina on its southern side on the edge of the Hadleigh Ray.

The eastern half of the island, together with the adjoining salt marshes and a larger area of adjacent mudflats, is now a nature reserve, leased to English Nature and managed by the Essex Wildlife Trust. This was the first part of the island to be transformed into a protected natural area when in 1974 Southend Borough Council rejected proposals for commercial development and issued a long-term lease for the land to what was then the Nature Conservancy Council (NCC). Leigh National Nature Reserve, as it became known, includes one of the best salt marsh areas in the Thames estuary and the mudflats surrounding the island provide exceptional feeding facilities for numerous species of marine birds. In conjunction with the neighbouring Southend-on-Sea Foreshore Local Nature Reserve which was designated in 1996, it provides one of the most important wildfowl and wading bird areas in Essex.

The mudflats around Two Tree Island are of international importance in terms of the large numbers of Brent Geese which arrive there in the early autumn to feed on the abundance of eel grass which is available. Rare types of seagull are also attracted, due in part to the proximity of the Leigh-on-Sea cocklesheds. Curlew, dunlin, mallard, redshank, ringed plover, shelduck, teal, widgeon and many other similar marine bird species can also be seen. On land, short-eared owls and marbled white butterflies are the main airborne attractions.

Remains of a redundant Edwardian sewage plant are still identifiable within the reserve, though largely overgrown, whilst the former rubbish tip (in use from 1936 to 1974) has all but disappeared. The island's history as a tip has surprisingly served to enhance its natural diversity by giving rise to a number of unusual and unexpected plants in the area, many of which would otherwise normally be alien to it. Hence fruit trees and daffodils can be seen alongside

Seawall, Two Tree Island

Causeway to the mainland, western end of Two Tree Island

more traditionally wild species such as sycamore and hawthorn. To the south of the island golden samphire, sea aster and sea purslane are all amongst the important saltmarsh plants on view.

The Two Tree Island reserve is one of the largest in the county, comprising in total some 634 acres - 170 acres of rough grassland and scrubland on the island itself, plus the surrounding saltmarsh, and a further 464 acres of mudflats. Its environmental importance has led to it being designated as a Site of Special Scientific Interest (SSSI) and it is a popular location for walkers and bird-watchers, with numerous nature trails both in the interior and along the seawall. A detailed information board at the entrance lists some of the species that can be seen within the reserve, whilst a bird hide and a Second World War pillbox (the latter at the easternmost tip) both provide good observation points over the natural attractions.

The western half of the island is also an important nature conservation site as it now forms part of the Hadleigh Castle Country Park (established in 1987). Its natural interest, however, is not yet quite as diverse or full grown as that in the nature reserve because landfilling continued later than on the eastern side and the land has not yet had time to reach its full potential. It largely takes the form of open grassland rather than the scrub of trees and bushes that makes up the eastern side.

Nevertheless, there is much of interest on the western half of the island, including, at the very western tip, an expansive lagoon which is home to a comparatively rare avocet population which returns to Two Tree every year to breed.

Just before the lagoon, on the northern side of the island, a causeway provides a link across the creek at low tide to a mainland seawall walk to Benfleet which enables visitors to join up eventually with the main portion of the country park.

Apart from its purely natural pursuits, the western half of the island is also home to a number of more formalised recreational activities. There is a circular track there for horse-riding, cycling and running and also a separate area which is used by a model aircraft club to fly its planes. Elsewhere, there are yacht anchorages in the creek between the island and the mainland and a marina on the southern side with a slipway into the Thames. Picnic tables are also provided, with views over the river.

Two Tree Island has never been occupied in great numbers by human beings, so it is rather short on documented history, even since the time of its reclamation from the sea in the 18th century. It did, however, enjoy (if that is the right word) a brief spell of national attention in the aftermath of the 1953 floods. Like neighbouring Canvey Island, Two Tree was severely flooded by the Great Tide but the numbers of people on the island were considerably smaller and the only ones to suffer there were two operators from the old sewage works who were temporarily stranded on the roof until they could be rescued. The acting chairman of Benfleet Urban District Council lived in Leigh at the time and it was the sight of Two Tree Island under water that first alerted him to the dangers of the tragedy which might be unfolding on Canvey Island further out in the Thames.

During the flood rescue operations the island was often referred to as Leigh Marsh Island, perhaps a more physically accurate description as the number of trees has increased considerably since whoever first gave the island its true name actually did so.

Administratively, the eastern half of the island lies in the Borough of Southend and the western half in the Borough of Castle Point, but this difference is not evident to the visitor on the ground.

Bridge to Two Tree Island leading towards the mainland

# THE ESSEX ARCHIPELAGO

The next group of islands along the coast to the east of Two Tree is the curious but sizeable grouping of six low-lying marshland islands at the confluence of the Rivers Thames and Crouch. Foulness, New England, Havengore, Rushley, Potton and Wallasea Islands are known collectively as the 'Essex Archipelago', though the term 'archipelago' is slightly misleading as the islands fit together almost like a jigsaw puzzle. "The whole area," according to one observer, "is more like a delta, but of which river is hard to judge."

An old island inhabitant told Essex author and wildfowler, James Wentworth Day, who visited the area in the 1920s, that "There ain't no islands hereabouts... leastways none what signify..." Nevertheless, Wentworth Day went on to write one of the most atmospheric accounts of the archipelago in his *Coastal Adventure*.

His description is repeated here to help set the scene.

"These islands [have] a curious, haunting fascination. Their treeless horizons, their immense spaces, the vision of haystacks and houses standing up bold out of the flat land, and the endless monotone of sheep's voices and birds' voices either appal you with their loneliness and desolation or lay such hands upon the heart that a man must return to the islands once he has known them... to sense the silence, to smell the sea winds, to hear the chant of birds and the endless, immemorial, secret chuckle of the tides. It is a prairie land of the sea, unlike anywhere else in England.

"There is a peace on these sea-marsh isles which no other part of England knows - the peace of immense spaces; of a great wash of sea and sky; of mile on mile with neither house nor man nor road; the voice of a thousand sheep crying like an aerial undertone in the silence; the gleam of the sun on dykes and sea and tide-bared flat, the thin music of a little running wind creeping like a mouse in the long grass; the cry and wheel of curlew and shank against the dawn sky."

This combination of immense beauty and stark loneliness gives these islands a special fascination all their own.

As Wentworth Day implied, all six islands are predominantly agricultural but unfortunately access to them as a group is somewhat restricted. Foulness is controlled by the Ministry of Defence (MoD) and New England and Havengore Islands, which are now joined to Foulness as one continuous 'super island', also come under the Ministry's jurisdiction. Access to all three is limited, to say the least, and very few people who do not live or work there have actually set foot

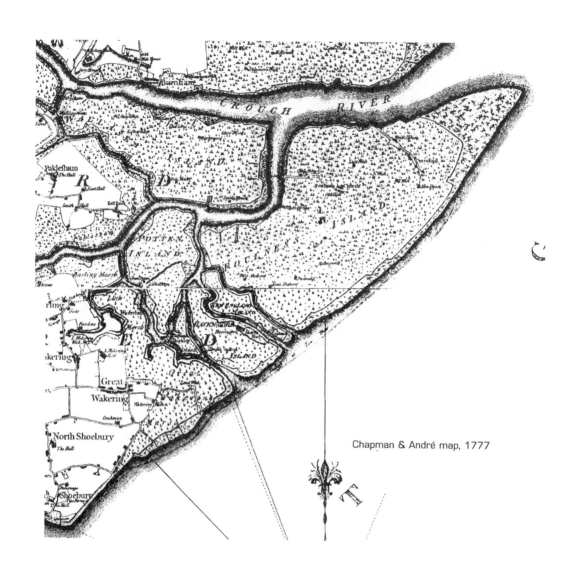

Chapman & André map, 1777

on them. Potton Island is also under MoD ownership, though the Ministry's activities have been scaled down there in recent years.

Access to Rushley Island, which is almost 100% agricultural, is more limited by its geographical position than by any MoD restrictions (though these have had their effect too). The island is bordered by Potton Island to the north west, Havengore Island to the north east and a combination of privately-owned agricultural land and an MoD checkpoint on the mainland to the south. There is, at least, a public footpath along the seawall to the south on the mainland which affords a good view of the island for those willing to take the walk.

Wallasea Island is without doubt the most easily accessible of the six, though even this has restrictions (imposed by geography and private farmland ownership), with only the north-western corner very much frequented by the public. There is a seawall walk along the northern and eastern sides of the island and Wallasea's position as the only one of the six to the north of the River Roach means that it has two significant rivers passing either side of it (the Roach and Crouch), so yachtsmen too are able to get a good view of it.

The Essex Archipelago is without doubt a curious but fascinating place.

Details of each island are given in the following chapters, starting clockwise with the largest and most well-known of the six - Foulness.

George & Dragon pub and St Mary's church, Churchend, Foulness

## FOULNESS ISLAND

*"...that strange island where no stranger is welcome, where all unknown faces are suspect..."*

JAMES WENTWORTH DAY, *Coastal Adventure*

The largest of the six islands in the Essex Archipelago is Foulness. With approximate dimensions of seven miles by five and an acreage of between six and seven thousand, it is in fact the largest island in Essex. Many mistakenly believe that this honour falls to Canvey, but the restrictions on access to Foulness, which has been controlled for years by the Ministry of Defence (MoD) and its forerunners, have led to many misconceptions about the place.

The name, according to Dr. Reaney, is derived from the Old English term 'fugla-ness', or "wild birds' ness [promontory]", though other sources claim it comes from 'fuhl-a-ness' ("muddy island's headland"), a Danish derivation.

Like Canvey, Foulness was owned and farmed until comparatively recently by inhabitants of mainland parishes adjacent to the island. Philip Morant's *The History and Antiquities of the County of Essex*, written in 1768, records that for years the island was divided up into the ownership of the six mainland parishes of Eastwood, Little Stambridge, Little Wakering, Rochford, Shopland and Sutton. Also like Canvey, Foulness did not initially have its own place of worship and islanders wishing to attend church had to travel across country to whichever mainland parish was responsible for their land. This system of mainland parish ownership lingered on in some respects for centuries - tithes, in fact, were still being paid to the mainland parishes in mid-Victorian times.

The island was first occupied, however, many centuries before the Victorians. Archæological evidence, including that excavated from a Romano-British burial mound (possibly similar to the larger tump on Mersea Island (see later)), has shown that Foulness was inhabited at least as early as Roman times. The discovery in 1848 of a large collection of pots at a site known as Little Shelford (some dating to the second century) provided much evidence to support this, whilst a number of so-called 'Red Hills', thought to be remnants of early salt-making facilities, give additional evidence of Roman occupation.

As at Canvey, the land and waters hereabouts have given up many Roman treasures over the centuries. Amongst the most remarkable, if it genuinely is Roman, must surely be the Broomway - a raised ancient trackway out in the sea running parallel to the coast about half a mile from it for some six miles from Wakering Stairs on the mainland to Fisherman's Head on the island.

Several tracks branch off this 'road' to farms on the island and for many centuries it was the only sure way of getting onto Foulness for those without a boat. It is thought that the track was built out in the sea, as opposed to on dry land, because the numerous creeks on the island made it difficult to construct a route over land, whereas a raised path situated on the relatively level mud surface out at sea could at least be built up and maintained whenever the tide was out.

The name, 'Broomway', comes from the hundreds of poles which mark the outer edges of the route, which are similar in appearance to the handles of garden brooms.

It was during the Great Tide of 1953 - which affected Foulness as badly as it did Canvey, though with nowhere near as great a loss of human life - that the Broomway proved its real value by providing the only safe route via which rescuers could reach the island's stranded inhabitants. A convoy of cattle trucks was used to evacuate not just humans but also a whole variety of farm animals, over 1,500 of which were ultimately rescued. Although providing a valuable access route to the island, the Broomway can also be an extremely dangerous place as it is completely covered at high tide and anyone unfamiliar with the route would be risking life and limb if attempting to use it at the wrong time. Many a tale is told on the island about those who mis-timed their journey and never returned to attempt the route again.

The argument behind the theory that the Broomway is Roman is based on the fact that a Roman road is known to have connected nearby Prittlewell with Wakering Stairs and that the quickest route from this area to the Roman fort at Othona, near Bradwell-on-Sea in Dengie Hundred to the north, would have been straight across the water from Foulness. A more likely alternative theory is that there was actually a Roman fort off Foulness itself which the Broomway once led to but which has now disappeared under the sea due to the well-documented rise in sea level which has taken place around this area of the coast over the centuries. These forts, built to defend the Roman Empire against Saxon invaders, and so known as 'Forts of the Saxon Shore', were generally constructed with equidistant spacing between them and the unequal gap between Othona and the next confirmed fort to the south at Reculver, Kent, suggests that there may well have been another at Foulness, halfway between the two. Proper excavation is really needed to confirm this as no evidence for military occupation of Foulness during Roman times has yet been found.

Apart from the Broomway, road access to the island was non-existent before 1922 when the government opened a new road to the military facilities.

St Mary's, Foulness

George & Dragon, Foulness

Until then, the only other method of access was to take the ferry. In the mid-19th century there were four ferries to the island - one across Havengore Creek (approximately where the bridge is now), one from Potton Island, one from Wallasea Island (which landed on Foulness at Monkton Barns hard) and one from across the River Crouch at Burnham. Foulness has historically had a good relationship with Burnham, which was geographically closer than Southend and was not difficult to get to by boat along the Crouch.

As with Canvey, it seems likely that Foulness (and the five other Archipelago islands) was originally part of the mainland and was formed as an island only as the sea level rose. The fertile coastal marshland to be found there made it a hugely valuable asset for farming purposes and, like the land at Canvey, it was from the earliest times used to provide pasture for cattle and sheep. The sale of dairy by-products from these animals helped to sustain the island's economy.

Soon, however, the pasture land was gradually replaced by fields given over to arable farming and the combination of an extensive programme of land reclamation (known as 'inning' in Foulness terminology) and more intensive use of available land ensured that arable farming eventually took over completely. Much of the land was looked after by tenant farmers and many of the white weatherboarded cottages which were built to house those people remain to this day. In respect of its feeling of apparent timelessness, Foulness has changed very little since this period.

The island is still predominantly agricultural, despite the MoD activity, and the largest developments are the hamlets of Churchend and Courtsend, which collectively house no more than a few hundred people. The well-known farmer and writer, Arthur Young, one-time secretary of the Board of Agriculture, visited Foulness on a tour of the county in the early 19th century and had much to say about the good quality of the island's soil. In 1972 wheat grown on Foulness by Belton Brothers (now, with Burroughs, one of the two major farming concerns on the island) won the World Championship at the Royal Agricultural Winter Fair in Canada - the first time the title had been won by a UK farm.

The practice of 'inning', referred to above, is of particular significance on Foulness since land reclamation began there before 1420, earlier than anywhere else in the county. The first seawalls were probably built in the 12th or 13th century, just protecting the existing land and saltings. The first major reclamation was at New Wick, where 220 acres were taken from the sea, but this was only one of a long line of extensive and highly successful land reclamation projects. These continued into the early 1830s when a 251-acre scheme was concluded. The geography at Foulness has been greatly affected by land reclamation - for example, a bay area known as Wakering Haven has now completely disappeared.

Naturally, all reclaimed land was highly valuable for agricultural purposes because of its superior quality and was therefore always much sought after. Claims that the Dutch were involved in the inning process have never been fully substantiated, although many people listed in the island's parish registers are shown as "seawallers" by trade and many of these came from Lincolnshire, where much fenland reclamation was undertaken by Dutch workers. There is, therefore, at least some circumstantial evidence to support the theory.

The promise of better quality land attracted many powerful landowners and parts of the island found their way into the ownership of a succession of well-known local families. These included the de Bohuns, the Boleyns and the family of the one-time Lord Chancellor, Lord Rich. The de Bohun family first held ownership of the island in about 1324 and it remained a part of their estates for many years. It was, in fact, Lady Joan de Bohun, in the late 14th and early 15th centuries, who was instrumental in establishing a permanent chapel on the island and securing the payment of church dues towards the upkeep of the chapel instead of to the appropriate mainland parishes which had hitherto benefited from the islanders' payments. This chapel lasted until the 1540s, when, under the ecclesiastical upheaval instituted by Henry VIII's dissolution of the monasteries, the chantry was dissolved and the chapel's land and possessions were confiscated. By 1550, however, fortunes had changed. Foulness was made a parish in its own right and the old chapel was replaced with a specially constructed timber-framed church. A hole was provided in the spire of this building to allow smoke from the vestry fire to escape. The nave roof was covered with red tiles, whilst inside the ceiling and walls around the sacrosanct area were plastered and the floor was bare earth.

In succeeding years this church played host to a number of unusual individuals and suffered as a result something of a rather chequered early history. In 1553, for example, its patron, Sir William Stafford, sold all the church bells except one to finance repairs to the seawall after severe flooding. He is reported to have justified his actions by saying that "the parish needs but one bell to call the islanders to prayer". Despite this defence, his act made him unpopular with the local witch, who allegedly cast a spell to cover all his land with mice as a punishment. Whether this deterred Sir William from indulging in further misdemeanours is not recorded, but it is known that he also sold four of the five bells of neighbouring Rochford's church for the same purpose!

Almost a century later, in 1642, at the start of the Civil War, Roboshobery

Dove, the incumbent at Foulness at the time, was a staunch Royalist. As most of Essex was Parliamentarian this made him extremely unpopular with the authorities and in 1644 he was summoned before a Maldon court as a result on charges of "drunkenness, conformity and affection to the King's cause". Not surprisingly, he was found guilty and, after several unsuccessful attempts to remove him, he was finally dislodged from the island's incumbency, although his wife, Sarah, was allowed to retain some of the benefits which were due to a man of his position.

Eight years later there was still some confusion about whether Foulness possessed a church or a chapel (apparently an important distinction), although it was noted at the time that the incumbent, Mr Goodeene (or possibly Goddiffe), was popular with his parishioners. The earliest surviving parish records of the island date from shortly after this time - 1695. Another notable survivor from this period is the 1698 gravestone of Jonas Allin - one of the earliest outdoor grave monuments in existence in Essex.

The timber-framed church was demolished in the 1840s because it was in need of extensive and costly repair and was becoming too small to accommodate the island's growing population. A new church was quickly erected, the money for it being raised largely by public subscription. A donation was also forthcoming from Trinity House, on condition that the new church was built with a steeple high enough to act as a landmark for shipping. This church, designed by William Hambley in a then fashionable Early English style, was dedicated on 3rd July 1853 to St Mary the Virgin. A lock-up cage also erected there for the safekeeping of wrongdoers was later used as a mortuary, though this latter practice was soon discontinued as most of the prostrate bodies did not fit properly into the cage and their owners' feet could often be seen sticking out onto the roadway!

Despite the inning and the seawall repairs financed by the sale of the church bells, the small but constantly growing population and its valuable agricultural land and animals were still very vulnerable to flooding and the threat of inundation was always a major disadvantage of living on the island. On 16th February, 1736, a particularly large tidal surge swept down the east coast and flooded the coastal areas from Lincolnshire to Kent. This surge, coming at the time of a full moon and accompanied by strong north westerly winds, followed a familiar pattern. Seawalls were broken down, agricultural land was destroyed and hundreds of people were made homeless. The February issue of the *Gentleman's Magazine* recorded that, amongst other areas, "the little Isles of Canvey and Foulness were quite under water, not a hoof was saved, and the inhabitants were taken from the upper part of their houses into boats". Both islands clearly suffered severe inundation - and not for the first or last time.

Foulness at this time and for many decades afterwards was a most unhealthy place to live, more so even than Canvey which at least had some protection from the elements by being sheltered in the Thames. In contrast, the geographical position of Foulness combined with its flat open aspect led to the exposure of both the island's inhabitants and their buildings to the bitter easterly winds coming in off the North Sea. It was once reported that the wooden buildings on the island were in danger of collapsing because the damp air was creeping into the joints and weakening them from the inside. The Board of Agriculture representative, Arthur Young, on his tour of the county in the early 19th century, reported that illness was almost a way of life there. "I asked, I believe, thirty persons if they had had agues [fevers]," he wrote afterwards, "and every one answered in the affirmative." J. R. Smith, writing about Foulness in 1970, recorded that "historians and chroniclers from the 16th century to the 19th century when writing about Foulness have always agreed on one thing - that it produced unhealthiness in Man". The island, he went on to write, with its rough, predominantly male inhabitants - including criminals escaping justice elsewhere - and its exposure to biting winds was nevertheless "capable of being made one of the most salubrious spots in the country".

Some would argue that even today the island is no place for the fainthearted. As recently as September, 1992, a massive hailstorm caused havoc on the island when stones up to two inches in diameter rained down, flooding roads, cutting power supplies and killing hundreds of seabirds.

Even without such freak events there are problems. A recent navigational handbook stated that "Maplin, Foulness and Buxey [nearby sandbanks] offer little of what is usually understood by land or sand - and in any case there is a good chance that they will be shrouded by one of the mists that haunts these parts so that there will be virtually nothing to see... and certainly nothing to look at even when you can see anything".

Military interest in Foulness began in the 19th century. In 1849 the War Department, as it was then, purchased some lands at nearby South Shoebury with a view to setting up a firing range there. The extensive sandbanks to the east of this area, which stretch for over 20 miles out to sea, later (from the 1870s onwards) proved to be ideal testbeds for the safe launching of projectiles. Shells could be fired out into the sands and then collected again when the tide was out. This practice, known as Over Water Recovery (OWR), continues to this day.

The range at South Shoebury provided a maximum firing opportunity of 6,000 yards, ostensibly taking projectiles to the mouth of Havengore Creek, although many landed further on.

Towards the end of the 1870s the increased firepower then available led to proposals to extend the firing range to 12,000 yards, but a dispute between the War Office and landowners meant that it was to be 1893 before the extra land could be acquired (though some long-range firing had been taking place since 1885). In 1889 the New Ranges, running east of Shoebury, were installed and the rest of Maplin Sands were acquired between 1900 and 1922.

Neighbouring Havengore and Rushley Islands were also acquired in 1902. The manor of Foulness (which covered some two-thirds of island) was purchased in 1915 (along with the adjacent New England Island) and thus was completed a sizeable purchase covering the entire local area. By 1918 the Department had bought up almost all of the remaining land on Foulness and by 1970 only the church and the rectory, a mission hall at the hamlet of Courtsend and the island's school were not owned by the Government. (Since then, the mission hall has been demolished, the church and school have closed and the rectory has been bought by the MoD.)

In 1915 a contract was placed for the supply of a Scherzer Rolling Lift Bridge across Havengore Creek, though this was not erected until 1919. Road construction commenced shortly afterwards, though the distant settlement of Courtsend was not reached until 1924. New England Creek, separating New England and Havengore Islands, was dammed at both ends. The same fate befell the southern end of Shelford Creek between New England and Foulness.

Despite this increasing military attention agriculture on the island still prospered, whilst the large numbers of seabirds which had taken to congregating there similarly refused to be put off by any firing - unless it came from the gun of a local wildfowler! Ironically, the natural features and extensive wildlife of Foulness have actually been preserved by the presence of the military establishments because the land has not been opened up to developers in the same way as much of the rest of the county. The strict control on access to the island has stifled its development in human terms but protected its charms in terms of natural wonders. The pace of life on the island is noticeably slower than on the neighbouring mainland - it really is like stepping back in Time.

It was during the 19th century, too, that a rather different kind of combat came to Foulness. The churchyard, like the area outside the *Lobster Smack* on

Canvey, was a favourite battle ground for illegal fist-fights. This was not, as one observer records, "because the loser could be more easily and speedily interred", but because it was next door to the inn, the George & Dragon, which apparently provided the changing quarters for the contestants and plenty of readily available liquid refreshment for everyone when the fight was over. A wall now separates the churchyard from the inn forecourt but this is a comparatively recent addition.

The island champion for many years was John Bennewith, the Foulness Farm Bailiff, who began fighting in 1810. His mother, Amelia, was landlady at the *George & Dragon* - presumably quite a convenient arrangement. Many fighters had nicknames and those belonging to some of Bennewith's opponents give some idea of the characters he encountered - 'Infant', 'Giant' and 'Bullock's Bones' were some of them. Perhaps it was one of these characters that Bennewith was said to have fought with one hand tied behind his back!

Without a doubt though, Bennewith's most famous fight was with a professional fighter called Leggatt, who was working as a plasterer in St Leonard's church, Southminster, on the other side of the River Crouch. The event seems to have been an excuse for a day of revelry. A specially commissioned ballad was written for the occasion, sung before the event in a tradition maintained by Irish fist-fighters by Bennewith himself. The contest was a hard one, Bennewith being knocked down several times throughout, until some words from his wife, who was acting as his second, miraculously instilled in him a new desire to win. This he duly did by fracturing some of Leggatt's ribs. Unfortunately, the words spoken by Bennewith's wife have not survived, but they must have been extremely persuasive! The contestants and their audience retired to the *King's Head* to celebrate - probably the one at Courtsend rather than the one in Southminster. The multi-talented Bennewith, reputed to be "one of the best dancers in his class", put on a celebratory display of footwork at the inn which allegedly complemented his earlier vocal talents. A legacy from these fighting times lives on on Foulness, for according to the well-known Rochford Hundred historian, Philip Benton, the island road known as Turtle's Wall or Walk was named after a contestant who was actually killed in a fist-fight.

The island had always been a rough place to live - an annual fair at the *King's Head* was discontinued because of disorderliness, whilst the formation of an association for the apprehension of horse stealers before the turn of the 19th century gives a rather large clue that that particular crime was fairly rife there.

It was not only horses that were stolen, however. The island was a paradise for smugglers. Its remote geographical location and the abundance of creeks and channels surrounding it meant that contraband could easily be brought ashore out of sight of the revenue men. Nothing escaped this pastime - even fresh water was once so scarce that it was valuable enough to smuggle. A well was sunk 92 feet in 1725 on Great Shelford marsh without success and it was not until 1829, on neighbouring Rushley Island, that landowner Francis Bannester found water at a depth of almost 500 feet. By 1889, however, wells had been sunk on 14 farms on Foulness.

A population of fist-fighters, horse stealers and smugglers was not perhaps the most likely to produce an avid churchgoing community, so it would need a man of special talents to take the living on the island if his parishioners were ever going to be encouraged to attend church. Foulness was actually very fortunate in having a succession of energetic and respected churchmen at the helm, perhaps none more so than Thomas Archer, who proved to be just the man to knock his rough congregation into shape.

Archer became a familiar figure on the island, riding everywhere on a horse he used for hunting and always smoking a distinctive white clay pipe. During his sermons he would leave the pipe in a niche in the porch, ready to be lit again when the service was over. He also dressed distinctively "in a blue frock-coat, white corduroy breeches, grey worsted stockings and a red nightcap". Unlike his largely illiterate congregation, Archer was well educated and, apart from his church tasks, he also found time to write a great deal of poetry under the pseudonym of 'Calliope'. A larger-than-life character, he was also known to indulge in fist-fights of his own with problematic parishioners and he once broke his leg whilst trying to jump the churchyard stile.

Foulness, with its abundance of wildlife, also gave Archer the opportunity to pursue his favourite sport of hunting and it was not unknown for him to wear his scarlet hunting jacket under his surplice if a service clashed with a hunt so that he could join in the chase immediately the event was over. During one marriage ceremony he even shouted the traditional hunting phrase, "Tally Ho!", when a fox which was being pursued by the hunt passed by the open door of the church.

There is no doubt that Archer thought highly of his own hunting ability and he is known to have deliberately chosen some of the most difficult routes in pursuit of his quarry in an attempt to show off his skill. On many occasions he lived to regret it, however, as he was often badly injured when trying to get his horse to jump some of the most 'unjumpable' obstacles.

The vicarage in Archer's time was a rather curious building with hidden passages and none of the usual bell facilities for attracting the attention of the servants. When wanting his wife, Susannah, he would beat the wall with a brush and call out her nickname - 'Pug'! A visit to the Archers' household must have been highly entertaining!

Archer died on 17th February, 1832, aged 82, and was buried in the chancel of his church, the forerunner of the present building. People came to his funeral from miles around, mourning the loss of a great character.

Sixty years later the potential loss of further Foulness lives was thankfully never realised when the floods of 'Black Monday', 29th November, 1897, swept in from the sea and covered some 2,000 acres of farmland. The floods lasted six days in some places, killing wild animals and large numbers of earthworms but no human inhabitants. The Foulness Commissioners, who had the responsibility of repairing any breaches in the island's seawalls and ensuring their upkeep, sought help from 300 soldiers stationed at Shoeburyness to assist with effecting the necessary repairs, but none was given as the officer in charge considered that the island was not in any real danger.

The Commissioners called in an engineer to assess the damage and he reported that cracks in the sea defences caused by a dry summer had allowed floodwaters to penetrate the walls and so undermine them, something which had happened to a greater or lesser degree all along the Essex coast. The walls were swiftly rebuilt a foot higher than their previous level, but the ruined agricultural land took over a decade fully to recover its legendary soil quality.

For a brief period in the 1920s and 1930s, after the new road was opened and before comprehensive military restrictions on access were put in place, Foulness enjoyed an unlikely tourist trade. People drove onto the island from the mainland across to the far seawalls to picnic on the beaches and watch the world go by on the ocean. Tea-rooms and the like were briefly established, but the industry was closed down virtually before it could get going. Some military activities were already in existence at this period - a Sound Ranging laboratory was built at Jerry Wood and a large building project near Courtsend (known as 'White City') was also embarked upon. (This had been intended to accommodate the Small Arms Experimental Establishment, which was relocating from Hythe, but in the event the move never materialised.)

The Second World War saw Foulness important on two grounds. Its military activities were one, whilst the extensive agricultural land played a significant part in home food production. Trials to identify the best method of carrying out the Normandy landings were amongst the many wartime activities that took place on the island. An anti-tank firing range was set up there and weaponry to combat Germany's V1 flying bombs was also installed.

After the war, Foulness took on a new appearance in places, with the construction of some new houses and the demolition of many more older ones. From the 1950s onwards an Atomic Weapons Research Establishment (AWRE) site was established (now closed) north-west of the island road and in 1963 an Environmental Test Centre (ETC) was opened north of Churchend. Today, the island is primarily used by the MoD as a "gunnery and explosives" centre.

Despite the increased protection afforded by the new seawall arrangements put in place following the Black Monday floods of 1897, the Great Tide of 1953 (the next major natural disaster to affect the island) flooded Foulness almost as severely as it did Canvey (which was nearly three square miles smaller than Foulness). There was, however, nowhere near so great a loss of life since the island's population was not even a tenth of that of its near neighbour. About 14 miles of wall, ironically raised and strengthened at vulnerable points for extra protection barely two years earlier, encircled the island to a height of 16½ feet above sea level. Although the water actually reached only 16 feet in height, the accompanying north-easterly winds gave it sufficient impetus to lift it over the walls, which soon collapsed under the pressure. The average height of land on the island is only seven feet above normal sea level (much of it is actually well below that height), so once the defences had been breached extensive flooding was always on the cards. Breaches in the seawalls eventually stretched for hundreds of yards, a serious mile-long breach on the north side of the island being the principal cause of extensive damage to both property and land.

As the outermost island of the Essex Archipelago Foulness was completely cut off from the mainland not just by a vast expanse of water but also by the hazards presented by five other submerged islands. It was impossible to tell where the land ended and the sea began. The island's most populated settlement, Churchend, was completely cut off from the mainland, some five miles distant. Up to 400 civilians were living on the island at this time, while on the night in question, in addition to the undisclosed numbers stationed on Government property, seven War Department police officers had been out in the open on patrol. Even so, the vast sheet of water and the huge landless expanse which it had introduced between the islanders and their potential rescuers made it impossible to begin a rescue operation straightaway without endangering the lives of those who were trying to do the rescuing.

Even when the operation finally did get into full swing there were many under-water obstacles to be negotiated before any success could be registered. The military nature of the island meant that, amongst other things, wire fencing and land-mines were hidden away under the waters. Amphibious vehicles, known as DUKWS, were initially thought to be the answer, but these could not explore further than Havengore Island because the road through the seawall to Foulness could not be found. The BBC broadcast a special message on the midnight news the day after the disaster struck, asking islanders to put lights in their windows so that rescuers could see where they were. A boat was sent out from Burnham-on-Crouch to the north of the island the following afternoon in an attempt to locate those who were stranded and take them off. Meanwhile, an army lorry convoy was using the Broomway to approach the island from the south. Some of the first photos of the effect of the Great Tide in Essex were recorded at Foulness and on neighbouring Wallasea Island at 12.30 p.m. on Monday, 2nd February, 1953.

Despite the length of time taken to effect a successful rescue attempt, some 362 people were eventually taken off the island, though six farmworkers volunteered to remain behind to tend the stranded farm animals that had not yet been rescued. Many of these, particularly the cattle, were herded on to the relatively high ground around St Mary's church where they could be kept in comparative safety. Although only three humans lost their lives in the tragedy in this area - two on Foulness and one on nearby Havengore Island - the loss of animal lives, particularly those of sheep and pigs, was higher than anywhere else in the county. The event was also to be a turning point in the island's modern history, as many islanders began to think seriously for the first time of moving to the mainland.

The floodwaters on Foulness took over three weeks to recede in some places and the land was ruined for many years for agricultural purposes. The effects of the flooding did, however, give rise to a number of subsequent biological surprises, with two botanists visiting the island the following year discovering giant specimens of the branched glasswort and annual seabright plants, three or four feet in height, which were clearly enjoying their new habitat.

The remoteness of Foulness caused many problems in effecting a successful rescue of the islanders in 1953 and the general lack of widespread public knowledge about the place has continually led to many strange stories springing up about the island. The local historian, Philip Benton, records for example that the place known as Lucky Corner was said to be the haunt of a ghostly apparition in the form of "a woman without a head". Elsewhere, the spectral remains of a wrecked sailing ship are alleged to be visible, crossing an area of reclaimed land on the island which was once water, whilst a pond on the island is said to be haunted by a serving maid who committed suicide by drowning after being thrown out of her master's house when he had made her pregnant. The island at one time even had its own witch, known locally as Old Mother Redcap, whose method of transport was by hurdle rather than by the traditional broomstick!

Although the effects of the Great Tide soon passed into history, Foulness was to make further national headlines 20 years later when, in 1971, nearby Maplin Sands was proposed as the site for a third London Airport and massive plans for an accompanying new motorway and a sea terminal were put forward. One proposal by the Thames Estuary Development Corporation involved the reclamation of some 18,000 acres of land. The scheme would have created a huge number of additional jobs but in the end, after much protracted discussion, the conservation argument won the day and the project was abandoned. The wild bird population on Foulness, then as now, had international significance and the Defenders of Essex Association, a union of conservationist groups, did all it could to advertise this fact. Some preparatory constructional work for the airport did actually take place and £3 million was rumoured to have been spent on it at the height of the exercise, when revised scheme after revised scheme was being drawn up for the area. One plan even included the construction of a runway across the islands of Havengore, New England and Foulness t accommodate jumbo jets. Thankfully, common sense ultimately prevailed over business interests and the project finally died a death in 1974, though speculative ideas for airport and seaport facilities are periodically, if tentatively, floated to this day.

The success of the Maplin Airport scheme would almost certainly have increased the island's population beyond all expectations but its failure meant that the number of civilian-inhabited houses was still the same in the mid-1980s as it was in the middle of the 19th century. The population peak was actually reached over 100 years ago, in the 1870s, when a total of 750 people lived on the island (ignoring government employees). But islanders here, as at Canvey, knew how to fight for their interests when developers were threatening to invade their community and they ultimately won the day.

The Maplin Airport scheme was not the first grand development project to be put forward for the Foulness locality. In common with Canvey, Foulness was considered by the Metropolis Sewage and Essex Reclamation Company as a likely place where sewage collected from the end of the Northern Outfall sewer could be piped, to enable the enrichment of land which could then be reclaimed from the sea. The plan centred on three main proposals, the first being put forward in 1861-2 when the idea of constructing a 44-mile long sewage conduit with branches to East Wick Head on Foulness and the mainland of Dengie Hundred was introduced. In later plans the Foulness part of the scheme became the primary objective and the Dengie part secondary, but a lack of financial backing meant that it never got off the ground. An advert for the project actually appeared in *The Times* newspaper, claiming 120 million tons of sewage could be used in this way every year and that the scheme would generate a net profit of some £650,000.

This project followed on from an earlier proposal by the South Essex Estuary and Reclamation Company to reclaim 30,420 acres of saltings and mudflats off the Essex coast, including Maplin and Foulness Sands, areas off Dengie Hundred and, further to the north, Mersea Island. The company's proposals were approved by an Act of Parliament in 1852 and almost £4,000 was spent on the construction of a 1.25 mile long causeway out from Sales Point and the digging of an accompanying creek, but opposition from local landowners and the traditional lack of financial backing led to the scheme folding.

The failure of the Maplin Airport scheme certainly guaranteed the future of the island's wildlife population, which has continued to thrive over the years despite, or rather because of, the presence of the Ministry of Defence and its predecessors. Large numbers of seabirds, some species comparatively rare elsewhere, live on or around the island, which has consequently become increasingly popular with ornithologists over the years. The Great Shellbanks at Foulness Point, a Site of Special Scientific Interest (SSSI), are a particularly important geographical feature. Made almost entirely of cockleshells and continuously being shaped and re-shaped by the actions of the wind and the tides, they are the largest of their kind in Europe and are therefore of international significance. The cockleshells emanate from cocklebeds further along the coast and in many places are formed into solid banks out in the sea which in turn form a low platform for birds to rest on at low tide. Many of these banks are centuries old.

The constantly changing nature of these shellbanks makes them unsuitable for all but a few plant and animal species but they are hugely popular with birds such as the common and little tern, the ringed plover and the oystercatcher. Little terns have also taken over a bank which was built as part of the Maplin Airport scheme, so much so in fact that it now houses one of the largest such colonies in Britain.   English Nature's draft site management plan for the Foulness SSSI (1997) identifies six species of international importance on the island (bar-tailed godwit, dark-bellied Brent geese, grey plover, knot, oystercatcher and redshank) and three of national importance (curlew, dunlin and shelduck). 30% of British and 15% of North West European Brent goose sightings are made in the areas between Canvey and Foulness Islands in the winter and counts of up to 20,000 have been made there.   The dwarf eel grass here on which they feed is the longest continuous stretch in Europe and the birds are consequently also protected by European Union directives.

Inside its seawalls, Foulness has some of the most interesting grazing marshes in Essex with a particularly rich selection of flowering plants.   In 1970 a comprehensive survey of the island by the Natural Environment Research Council revealed that over 200 species were present in some areas.   As for mammals, Foulness is home to large numbers of hares, which are comparatively rare elsewhere.   The MoD takes its conservation responsibilities seriously, balancing operational requirements with English Nature's plans.

During the Maplin Airport campaigns 13 conservation groups and local authorities put forward a proposal for the island's transformation into a huge recreational area for use by the general public, but the Government's requirement for it to continue as a weapons testing area put paid to that suggestion and, in all honesty, probably served to retain it as a more natural wildlife area.   In contrast, much of Man's important architectural contribution to the island has been destroyed by the Government, as many of the older buildings have been demolished.   Amongst the  more important ones remaining are:   New House Farm, a timber-framed three-storeyed weatherboarded structure built in the mid-17th century; the *George & Dragon* inn, built c.1650-1700 as three separate cottages; Priestwood and Rugwood farmhouses, dating from about 1700 and 1750 respectively (a building stood on the site of the former in at least 1509); and the island's manor house, known as Old Hall, which is one of the few Victorian buildings of note.   Quay Farm, of 1811, hides inside it an earlier 17th century timber-framed building.   Also significant is Ridgemarsh Farm dating from 1687 but featuring timbers from over a century earlier, which was almost certainly the first brick building on Foulness and is therefore sometimes referred to as 'Bricked House'.   Bricks were brought in from the brickfields at Stambridge (on the mainland) until about 1830, but by the 1880s they were coming in by barge from Shoeburyness. Tree Farm (often called 'The Dutch House') was built in 1687-8 by wool traders, whilst Signal House, of about 1800, was part of a chain of signal stations stretching from

Yarmouth to Southampton erected in preparation for the expected Napoleonic invasion. A windmill dating from the same period which was to be used to provide milled flour locally if the country was invaded was never used extensively and was demolished during or just prior to the First World War. Fortunately, many of the buildings which were once scheduled for demolition by the MoD have been saved for posterity thanks to the Foulness Conservation & Archæological Society. The society has a small conservation room at the *George & Dragon* and is currently negotiating for the lease of the old school, with the aim of providing a larger and better display area for its exhibits.

A pass is generally required to visit Foulness these days, though certain events - such as the annual cycle ride, flower show/fête and ploughing match (when held on the island) - are thrown open to visitors. It is certainly worth trying to visit if at all possible - it is just like stepping back in Time to a curious landscape where war and peace seem to co-exist quite happily. Older island residents may have seen a few changes (more cars, the mechanisation of agriculture, a reduction in the number of youngsters staying on the island) and lost a few facilities (a pub, a shop, the school and the church have all closed in recent years), but Foulness remains a unique place in which to live and work. The church was closed as recently as 1999 but there is a campaign under way to try to get it reopened.

The Ministry of Defence, through its Defence Evaluation & Research Agency (DERA) seems set to continue to control the island (and its smaller neighbours) for the foreseeable future, though the government's Strategic Defence Review may well have an effect on exactly what goes on there. There has been some speculation about whether the MoD will depart the island altogether at some period and whether that will mean it is opened up and developed. Most local people, both on and off the island, appear to be against this, having seen what large-scale development has done to nearby, once similar-sized communities on the mainland. Occasional speculative proposals do crop up, however - a plan was put forward in 1998, for example, for an electricity-generating wind farm on the island.

Life on Foulness may well have its restrictions, but in a place where everyone knows everyone else and where a huge Ministry of Defence presence dominates the island, a relatively crime-free environment and a beautiful natural landscape must be great selling points.

## NEW ENGLAND ISLAND

*"...that desolate isle..."*

JAMES WENTWORTH DAY, *Coastal Adventure*

New England Island is, or, perhaps more accurately, was, the smallest of the six principal islands in the Essex Archipelago. Following the damming of Shelford and New England Creeks during the construction of the government road from the mainland to Foulness Island in the 1920s it was joined irretrievably to both Foulness and Havengore Islands, which collectively now form one big island land mass. This merger with Foulness Island on one side and Havengore Island on the other has meant that New England Island itself has lost much of its original individual identity.

Even before this, however, it seems that the identity of New England Island was never that distinctive - it is one of the few islands in the county for which apparently no trace can be found of precisely how it got its name. Eighteenth century author, Philip Morant, dismisses it in a sentence as being home to "nothing remarkable". The later Rochford Hundred historian, Philip Benton, records in a little more depth that the areas of land on New England Island were flooded twice "in the memory of man" (he was writing in 1867), with 300 sheep being drowned during the first inundation.

The island's tendency for sudden flood was no doubt accentuated by the fact that, uncharacteristically for the Essex coastline, areas of it extended out into deep water and then fell sharply. There was no shallow seabed over which tides could advance gradually and the incoming water could often catch people unawares. Although this geographical feature appears to have altered over the centuries so that inundation does not occur so suddenly as it once did, the island is no less prone to flooding that its near neighbours. Indeed, in the Great Tide of 1953, it was completely under water. Some 50 years earlier, following the 'Black Monday' floods of November, 1897, the island had to be completely abandoned until long after the floodwaters had receded.

For many years the property of the mainland parish of Little Wakering, just over two miles away, New England Island seems to have been one of the area's principal breeding grounds for sheep, which explains Benton's concern for the sudden loss of 300 of them in one go. Wool, skins (for parchment), meat, butter, milk and cheese were all sent off to market from these marshland areas, though the advent of new agricultural methods in the late 18th century led to some decline in this prosperous trade. A proposal to increase island income by the laying and cultivation of winkle-beds, which could perhaps have become as profitable as the Essex oyster trade, never came to fruition.

In the 16th century New England Island was in part-ownership of the powerful Lord Rich, indicating that it was highly regarded even outside the immediate locality. The administrators at London's St Bartholomew's Hospital were also once important landowners on the island and it was they who were largely responsible for ensuring regular and adequate maintenance of the island's seawalls.

The Ministry of Defence (MoD) took over New England Island in 1915 when it completed the substantial purchase of large areas of neighbouring Foulness. Just under half of it was let for grazing initially, the land being farmed, like that of Havengore Island, which was in a similar situation, by Caleb Rayner Ltd., a firm based locally at Great Wakering on the mainland.

Today, no-one lives on New England Island and MoD restrictions effectively prevent any free access to it. Visitors to Foulness pass over it along the MoD road almost without being able to identify it separately as an island in its own right. At least if the time-capsuled lands in these parts do ever become publicly accessible once again, their exploring visitors will be able to discover a New England in more ways than one.

Ridgemarsh Farm, Foulness

# HAVENGORE ISLAND

*"...fogs were all too prevalent and biting wind swept in across the marshes..."*
LILY JERRAM-BURROWS, *The Smaller Islands of the River Crouch*

Much like all the other islands in this corner of the county, Havengore Island has never had the kind of climate that encourages inhabitation. The building of the road on to Foulness by the Ministry of Defence's forerunner in the 1920s and the damming of New England and Shelford Creeks certainly made it easier for those without a boat to reach the island, but most of these new visitors were bound for the larger island beyond and the population on Havengore itself never substantially increased.

A few military trials were actually carried out on Havengore even before the road was built. The government acquired the island (and the adjacent Rushley Island to the west) in 1902 (over a decade before the Foulness purchase) and a few tests were carried out towards the end of the First World War. More took place in the 1920s and 1930s.

Activity on Havengore - and at neighbouring New England Island (between Havengore and Foulness) - increased substantially after 1937 to include the development of AA 'Z' rockets and the carrying out of some Home Office trials leading up to World War Two. These included an examination of the best ways of tackling oil storage fires (very useful in the Blitz) and a study of the effects of bomb explosions in close proximity to Anderson shelters. Both islands were subjected to a range of other trials after the war was over.

The building of the new road effectively joined Havengore and New England Islands to the much larger Foulness and the three have since been treated almost as one. A lifting bridge spans the gap between Havengore and the mainland - boats are still allowed to sail through the creek there on their way from the River Thames to the River Roach (weapons testing and tides permitting) - but access to the island itself is as severely limited as that to the more high profile Foulness Island a mile or so up the road.

Funnily enough it is the numerous creeks around this part of the coast that offered yachtsmen of old the haven from the seas from which the island takes the first part of its name. The second part derives from the ever-present mud which is often visible in these highly tidal areas (referred to in Old English as 'gor'). On the neighbouring mainland the similarly named Haven Point is all that remains of a once-lengthy sandy spit which projected out into the Thames estuary until at least the first decade of the 19th century. The old parish of

Havengore, now no longer in existence, was known in the 13th century as 'Havenemersche', though it later became 'Havengor' and 'Havingor' before reaching its current state of literary development.

Nowadays the creeks around Havengore Island are still important recreational waters for leisure-time yachtsmen, but the working nature of the area has been considerably reduced from what it was a hundred years or more ago. In the 19th century fleets of barges were used around the creeks to transport cargoes from the nearby Wakering brickfields to London and to bring back city rubbish to burn in the  kilns and ashes to mix with the native brickearth for the production of yet more bricks.  Before the bridge onto Foulness was built, the barges would tie up at a place known as Mill Head, which was a specially constructed, mud-lined dock where they could stop to be loaded or unloaded as appropriate.  These barges could carry up to 45,000 bricks at a time.

In the 1860s there were two farms on Havengore Island.  According to the local historian, Philip Benton, the quality of the land on these was "far superior" to that on neighbouring Rushley Island but attracted a lower tithe rate, so it must have been an enticing proposition to the would-be farmer.  As with several other Essex islands the land on Havengore was once under the control of a number of mainland parishes but by Victorian times the island had been made a parish in its own right (only for parish status to be lost again - to Foulness Island - once the road on to Foulness had been constructed).  In Benton's time there were about 25 inhabitants on Havengore Island and this in fact was probably the most that it has ever supported at any one time.

After the road to Foulness was built in the 1920s the agricultural importance of Havengore Island soon began to decline and within 30 years it was nearly killed off altogether.  In January and February 1953, when the floods of the Great Tide struck this part of the coast, the only permanent residents there were the sole remaining farmer and the Havengore bridge-keeper and their respective families.

The lives of the former were saved by the alertness of a military policeman from 'Taylor's Hut' Police Lodge, a two-storeyed, flat-roofed concrete building, from which access to Foulness was controlled.  Unfortunately this act of heroism on the part of the policeman was not rewarded as, after alerting the farmer to the trouble and returning to Taylor's Hut to report back to Headquarters, he was overcome by the floodwaters and was sadly drowned. The bridge-keeper and his family spent the night trapped in their home before being rescued the following afternoon by an amphibious DUKW.  Water on

Havengore Island rose to eight feet in depth, but fortunately, unlike neighbouring Foulness, its population was small and so therefore was the corresponding loss of life.

This part of the country had always been considered rather exposed and inhospitable since long before 1953 and the marshes and the islands of Rochford Hundred were renowned until the late 19th century for their unhealthiness and their susceptibility to severe biting winds. Agues or fevers were typical here, as at Foulness. So much so, in fact, that Benton recorded (in 1867) that "the ague hung on every bush". Coughs, colds and consumption were all run-of-the-mill illnesses for inhabitants in these lands and a local gipsy woman called Mrs. Print made plenty of money selling 'cures' for the various island diseases.

Happily, by the turn of the 20th century, there was much improvement. Fresh water supplies, such as those discovered at Rushley Island (see later), were becoming more readily available and the removal of many of the trees and bushes which had been responsible for attracting germ-carrying insects led to a considerable improvement in the air quality on Havengore Island and in most of the surrounding areas of the Rochford Hundred.

Though unhealthy, Havengore saw much activity in the 19th century and was actually the property at one time or another of a number of significant local landowners. These included Lady Olivia Sparrow (Lady of the Manor at Leigh-on-Sea) and James Tabor (Lord of the Manor of Rochford), whose family have owned large areas of Rochford Hundred for many centuries.

This period also saw a great deal of smuggling activity, the maze of creeks and islands being ideal for the night-time smuggling of contraband by those who knew the area. In 1857 a concentrated anti-smuggling effort led to two old naval hulks being stationed in the area as river blockades. One of these was allegedly the *Beagle* - the ship in which the famous naturalist, Charles Darwin, made his legendary 'evolutionary' voyage.

After the smuggling phase had died out, Havengore Island found itself in the frontline of another, far more serious conflict - World War Two. A Spitfire crash-landed on the island in the first 18 months of the war, whilst a Hurricane fighter also came down there in 1942. Fortunately, neither of the two pilots was seriously injured. The washing up on the island of the body of a German airman showed how close the enemy were coming to their targets, whilst a similar find of the body of a merchant seaman also demonstrated that, war or no war, there was still a great deal of activity going on in and around the River Thames.

The dropping of bombs and the presence of the MoD did not, however, discourage the wildlife on Havengore Island, as prevalent here, comparatively-speaking, as it is on the much larger Foulness Island next door. Hare coursing was once very popular on Havengore, illustrating the prevalence of those animals there, but one of the most interesting wildlife stories comes from the time of the English Civil Wars when a sudden and inexplicable growth in the ant, rat and mouse population led to such severe destruction of the native grassland that the cattle and sheep which the land was supposed to be supporting could not get enough food and many of them consequently died. The insects and rodents only lasted a year, however, by which time an equally surprising sudden growth in the island's owl population was responsible for their being hunted to virtual extinction. No-one seems to know what happened to the owls!

Today, agriculture on Havengore Island has seen something of an upturn and beans, linseed, peas and wheat are all farmed on its 700 acres.

Havengore Bridge

Havengore Farm

# RUSHLEY ISLAND

*"Rushley is loneliest of all those islands [in the Essex Archipelago]... No boat sails to it from month's end to month's end. No man visits it but its farmer-owner from the mainland, or the cattle-dealer with his chequebook, ready to buy. Rushley lies alone, untouched, forgotten."*

JAMES WENTWORTH DAY, *Coastal Adventure*

Forty years on from Wentworth Day's observations of Rushley quoted above the island has changed very little. It is almost certainly the least visited island in the whole of the Essex Archipelago. The surrounding Ministry of Defence islands of Potton and Havengore (north-west and north-east respectively) and the adjacent mainland (to the south) which plays host to both MoD land and private agricultural activity, effectively act as a barrier to access from any angle of approach.

There is a ford across the creek to the island at low tide, but this is not open to the public. However, a public footpath along the seawall on the mainland to the south provides a surprisingly good view of the island, whose agricultural interior seems hemmed in by its higher seawalls. Yachtsmen can get a little closer, but with just one building - a modern barn - rising up out of the flat landscape, the island still looks lonely even from the river.

This atmosphere of isolation is a far cry from the Rushley of 200 years ago, when a local entrepreneur foresaw a great future for the island and set about trying to make his dreams come true. John Harriott was the man in question and in 1781 he embarked on a plan to enclose the whole island with three miles of seawall to put the highly fertile land within it to potentially prosperous agricultural use. A farm and several wells were constructed and Harriott's work on Rushley soon received national recognition, culminating in the presentation of a gold medal by the Society for the Encouragement of Arts and Sciences for all that he had done. Harriott was also offered the chance to meet the king and receive congratulations in person for having extended the latter's territory, but he courteously declined the offer. The transformation of Rushley from an island which it had been claimed could actually be sailed over at certain states of the tide into a great agricultural prospect was quite an achievement, but unfortunately for its owner there were to be many problems in store.

The 200-acre island had cost Harriott just £40 to buy, but the high cost of reclamation, increased by unreliable contractors, and his own inexperience in managing the land, meant that it was several years before any return on his investment could be seen. He soon realised that the newly-reclaimed land had been ploughed far too soon as his crops continually failed to produce anything substantial. But Harriott was not one to give up without a fight and by 1790 his persistence with improved farming methods led to the crop which was produced that year being valued at a respectable £600.

Even so, the entrepreneur seemed dogged by disaster. His house was destroyed by fire and in 1791 a tide which was 12 inches higher than any other within living memory at the time rose over his seawall by as much as eight inches and completely flooded the island. The necessary drainage works were soon completed, but Harriott was already in debt because of the early failure of his initial investment and he had no money left either to carry out the necessary repairs to the seawall or to stand biding his time while the land was recovering. He had no choice this time but to abandon his ambitions for the island and he elected instead to seek his fortune in America, leaving Rushley behind him to fend for itself.

Though undoubtedly one of the most colourful, Harriott's period of occupation was not the first such inhabitation of Rushley. Evidence of Roman occupation has surfaced and there have been many claims, the most notable by Rochford Hundred historian Philip Benton, that a number of Roman burial tumuli exist on the island. Without a proper survey and supporting archæological excavations to back up these arguments, there can be no conclusive proof either way.

What is certain is that the island was known by the 16th century, when the names 'Russhleye' (first recorded 1576) and 'Russheley' (1578) were apparently in common use, along with those of 'Russele' and 'Russeleye', but the derivation of the island's name is not clear.

Needless to say, the flooding of 1791 which finally defeated Harriott and all his schemes was not the last battle with the elements which Rushley had to fight. The island suffered as much as its larger neighbours during the Great Tide of 1953, whilst in January, 1881, during a particularly severe winter, snow and ice were the main threats, with men lost out on the marshes for days and many livestock animals being killed by the cold. The creeks around Rushley and the neighbouring islands were actually frozen over in many places and carts could be driven across them with ease.

Three years later the island suffered another inundation and a number of haystacks were carried away down New England Creek and out into the Thames estuary.

Over the years it seems that some land may have been lost to the island as a result of extensive and recurring flooding, as Benton, writing in 1867, made observations that traces of sea defences, possibly some of Harriott's, could be seen in the mud outside what were then the island's newest seawalls. Rushley was clearly still in occupation at this time, being used, amongst other things, for grazing, and there was fresh water available here earlier than in many other coastal areas, thanks largely to the efforts of the island's industrious 19th century owner, Francis Bannester.

In the 1930s pregnant cows from Rushley were often taken inland to Home Farm in Great Wakering when they were about to give birth, but one particular animal always returned to the island of her own volition to have her baby on what she obviously considered was her home.

It is not just cows that are associated with Rushley. The local racehorse trainer and one-time Rushley owner, Frank Threadgold, once bred a horse which he named after the island. Born in 1976 she was a bay mare with horse-racing parents called Crooner and Vicki Ann. She was later trained at the famous Newmarket track by Mr. H. C. Westbrook and was entered as a two-year-old for four races, mainly over a distance of six furlongs, between September and November, 1978. These took place at Yarmouth, Lingfield (twice) and Doncaster.

Unfortunately she was not a tremendously successful racehorse, finishing, at best, second from last in all these races, and she was retired for breeding purposes back into the ownership of the Threadgold family at Southend-on-Sea, who have farmed land at nearby Great Wakering since the 1930s. Sadly, she did not prove to be too successful at breeding either, although she did have one colt, a bay called Tudor Rhythm, in 1980, which was never raced. In 1987 she was officially retired from stud and disappeared from the record books.

The future for Rushley Island is unclear. There has been talk of the Ministry of Defence extending its operational activities to the island and if that were to be the case then the degree of human involvement with Rushley would certainly be increased. Its most likely role in the foreseeable future, however, would seem to be to continue as agricultural land and a 'buffer zone' between the MoD's Foulness activities and the residential mainland. Many would argue that Rushley is best left like that and as James Wentworth Day described it after the war - "alone, untouched, forgotten". Mother Nature would be sure to take better care of it than would Mankind.

## POTTON ISLAND

*"It was as lonely a life as any man could lead anywhere in the British Isles... And this within fifty miles of London, within a dozen miles of the stupendous seaside metropolis of Southend."*

JAMES WENTWORTH DAY, *Coastal Adventure*

Potton Island, like most of its neighbours in the Essex Archipelago, is still subject to Ministry of Defence restrictions. The MoD, however, has not been active on the island since the early 1990s and the main activity there today is farming.

The island, roughly pear- or diamond-shaped in appearance, with dimensions of two miles long by at most one mile wide, is the most westerly of the five islands in the Essex Archipelago south of the River Roach and is situated about a mile to the north of the mainland village of Great Wakering. The only access to the island is through Great Wakering Common, though it is probably best viewed, at least by those approaching by land, from the seawall footpath on the mainland to the south-west or from across the River Roach at Paglesham Eastend.

The name, 'Potton', is thought to come from the personal name, 'Pott(a)', perhaps a former landowner in the area, though the north country dialect word 'pot', meaning a deep hole, especially one in the bed of a river, would seem to be more appropriate here. There is also a story that a family named Potton living in Rochford Hundred during the 19th century either gave or received their name to or from the island, but the truth of this seems questionable.

Other names have included 'Pottyng(e)' or 'Pottyngore' (1419) and 'Pottingwick' (1612), whilst 13th century references to 'Great' (or 'Magna') and 'Little' (or 'New') Potton would appear to indicate that the central lake on the island was once large enough for the northern- and southern-most parts of the island to be considered almost as two separate entities. Indeed the local historian, Philip Benton, records that the island was once clearly divided into two distinct areas - two farms, known as Great and Little Potton, which were actually, for administrative purposes, located in separate parishes (those of Great and Little Wakering respectively).

The occupation of Potton Island, like the occupation of many coastal areas and islands in the county, dates back a long way. Finds of Neolithic axes and a Bronze Age palstave, plus the presence of a Roman 'Red Hill', indicate a long period of human inhabitation of many centuries. In the 5th and 6th centuries

Old MoD buildings, Potton Island

The bridge to Potton Island

Rushley Island, with Havengore Bridge in background

the geographical spread of the island may actually have been larger, as some of the saltings which today surround it may once have been dry land.

In the late 19th century farming on Potton Island was extensive. "Sheets of golden corn" stretched across the flat land. James Wentworth Day records that the island then swarmed with rabbits and hares, partridges and wild duck, its central lake being particularly popular with wildfowlers as a place for widgeon, mallard, teal, pochard and shelduck. Benton, writing in 1863, declares that at this time there were about 700 acres of farmland in Great Potton and 300 in Little Potton, the latter being the oldest part of the island, the former of the highest elevation.

"The cultivation," he wrote, "is principally carried on by single men whose habits may be grasped when numerous fights take place amongst themselves in Harvest time, and upon disputes with their master, the latter has been known to barricade himself in his own house."

One landowner of this period, "a gentleman, formerly a Whitechapel butcher, who pursued plans with respect to agriculture quite foreign to the ideas of his contemporaries", introduced a series of unusual experiments on the island. These included: the careful cultivation of black grass, which was fed to the ducks on the 'gentleman's' pond; the damming of water furrows in winter to preserve the water in case a dry summer was just around the corner; and the fattening of hogs on mustard seed in order, apparently, to give a flavour to the pork. An attempt was also made to fill up the creek to provide a causeway which would make access to the island easier, but boat owners who wanted to use the creek and oyster fishermen who saw their catch being eroded quickly caused this unnamed 'gentleman' to think again. Needless to say, few of these ideas outlasted the traditional ways.

The peace of Potton Island was suddenly altered, however, in 1884, when that constant island enemy, the sea, spilled over the walls, destroying the crops and drowning many of the wild animals which lived there. The rabbit population was a particularly bad casualty. The island is bisected by numerous drainage channels or rills and the only two buildings at this time - the farmhouse and a shepherd's cottage - were completely surrounded by water. The damage done to the land by this inundation meant that it could be used for nothing but pasture for many years afterwards. There were some proposals in the 1890s to use the island's clay for brick manufacture, while the creeks around it, particularly to the east and in the Roach, were put to use as oyster beds.

In the years before the First World War, the island retained its popularity with wildfowlers and was made a little more habitable by the introduction of an artesian well. There were even some plans in 1905 to develop it as a resort, with fancy suburban names such as the "Arcadian Beach Estate", but these came to nothing. Interestingly, two members of the Hester family were amongst those who actually parted with some money for development plots - perhaps they were related to the contemporary Canvey Island developer, Frederick Hester?

In 1909 the whole of the island was bought by the well-known Essex farming firm of Strutt & Parker and Great and Little Potton were united as one farm for the first time for many years. During the First World War 12 German prisoners and 12 conscientious objectors were put to work on the land and shortly after this the old area of Little Potton alone was said to be able to accommodate 12 teams of horses and 24 men on its arable fields!

In the 1920s Potton Island was described as a "great treeless prairie, ...flat as a board" - not much different from any of the other islands in the Essex Archipelago!

The farmhouse and the shepherd's cottage were still there, whitewashed, tiled and wooden-beamed, protected from the tides by seven miles of seawall, but there were still no roads and the only trees on the whole flat expanse were the plum trees in the farmhouse's garden. It probably looked much like an uncultivated, smaller version of how neighbouring Wallasea Island appears today. The once numerous wild rabbit population had still not recovered from the devastating effects of the 1884 flooding, but hares were present in great numbers. Partridges and duck were still popular with the wildfowlers, but the most unusual sight on the island at this time was surely the "huge blue animals, looking like Persian cats, which one startled sometimes from reed-beds and tussocks of rough grass". These, unbelievably, were non-native Angora rabbits, which had survived as a legacy from an incredible, unsuccessful fur-farming experiment which had been carried out by a previous inhabitant on the island. Perhaps it was the unnamed 'gentleman' referred to above ... ?

Drinking water was not available on Potton at this time and the island's sole inhabitants, the shepherd and his wife, had to make a twice-weekly visit to the mainland to collect a barrel of drinking water which was left specially for them on the other side of the creek on the edge of the Great Wakering cattle-marshes.

By the 1940s, however, agriculture on Potton Island was well on its way to being successfully re-established, thanks largely to the entrepreneurial activities of A. H. Philpot & Son, who took over the island in 1937 and set about reclaiming land and re-introducing crops. Uneven ground was levelled and virtually the entire island was planted with new grassland or used as arable land. 350 cattle, 200 sheep and at least 1,000 pigs were also introduced, though unfortunately most of the latter were killed off by swine fever. The cattle, often brought from Wales, were walked to the island all the way from Shoeburyness railway station.

In addition, the buildings were greatly modernised and electricity was introduced to go with the water supply which had been laid on from Bentalls farm at Little Wakering Wick a couple of years earlier. Drainage was improved, bathrooms were put into the farm cottages and a telephone line was laid underground across the creek. The roadway across Wakering Common was also made properly passable for the first time.

Three families lived there during this period and the island had its own Home Guard, whose members were no doubt often called to duty as some 250 bombs fell on Potton during the war, usually as a result of planes off-loading their unused payloads on the way back from London. The body of a German airman was washed ashore during the war years and this was quickly taken to the mortuary on the mainland in Rochford to be dealt with there. Six Italian prisoners-of-war were also put to work on the land there. Their tasks included the construction in 1946 of a 'hardway' across the creek for use at low-tide, which replaced an earlier hardway and, before that, a raft hand-pulled by ropes which was used to ferry animals and materials across from the mainland (though sometimes the animals were swum across). Though no human lives were lost on Potton Island during the hostilities, a number of sheep and cattle were unfortunately killed by a direct hit on their enclosure.

It was not just the Germans who were enemies. During one night in 1944 some 400 chickens and numerous sheep and lambs were stolen by unidentified thieves who made their approach and escape by boat under the cover of darkness.

As mentioned above, animals and materials were generally transferred on and off the island by boat, though special 'peatways', hard roads made of compacted oyster and mussel shells, had historically been laid down to take the weight of the farm waggons which could cross at low tide. A ferry which once served Potton Island from the mainland at Fleet Head to the south west was withdrawn from public service once the MoD took over the island.

Eight years after the war the floodwaters of the 1953 Great Tide trapped 11 people on the island and a 40-yard breach in the seawall led to the resulting influx of water causing much damage to the crops and land. All the inhabitants were together in the farmhouse and, despite the flooding, all but two of them (an old couple who refused to leave) were evacuated by boat on the Sunday midday tide (the midday after the night of flooding). The old couple did eventually come off at midnight when equipment was brought on to the island to help a flock of 450 stranded sheep. The animals were 'swum' off the island across the water to the mainland at Wakering Common, whilst the humans were taken to the home of their employers at Writtle Park, near Chelmsford, to be looked after there.

In all there were 11 breaches in the seawall on Potton Island, compared to just three on neighbouring Rushley Island, but the close proximity of Potton Island to the mainland and the ease of access to it meant that 70% of those breaches had been made secure within a week of the flooding, whilst at Rushley, which was inaccessible except at high water, none of the breaches had been repaired.

The severely flood-damaged land never had the chance to return fully to cultivation. In 1955 the MoD extended its activities from the adjacent Foulness Island and established a Blast & Fragmentation Range there as part of its Proof & Experimental programme. Activities included the testing of controlled explosions in cars, the knowledge gleaned from which was put to good use in sorting out bomb problems in Northern Ireland.

The local planning authority objected to the proposal at the time on the grounds that "the noise caused by gunfire and explosions would engender shock and alarm in the nearby residents and would also result in the loss of more excellent agricultural land and of natural amenities". It was overruled by the government and all public access was immediately restricted. Even so, some 80% of the island was leased out by the Ministry as farmland and the farmhouse was retained for use by the farm manager. As with Foulness, the Ministry's arrival also provided improved road access to the island and its first bridge, which soon made the nearby 1946 hardway redundant.

Today, in the post-Cold War climate of European peacefulness, the MoD has temporarily brought a halt to its activities on Potton, though access to the island remains restricted. Grazing and arable farming are the main activities there now, with farm buildings and associated cottages on the west of the island and redundant MoD buildings still dotted about to the north and south. Wildlife, too, is flourishing: hares, rabbits, foxes and plenty of birds, notably avocets, all live there in abundance. Crops grown include wheat, beans and rape and there is some set-aside. Friesian heifers from Dollyman's dairy farm in Wickford are also reared on the island. The whole of the 1,000 acres is usually run by just two men - a result of mechanisation and improved farming methods and a far cry from the 24 men in work there just after the First World War.

In MoD terms, despite occasional interest, the main role of Potton Island now (like Rushley and Havengore/New England Islands) appears to be to provide a 'buffer zone' between Foulness and the mainland.

The mainland entrance to MoD land at Potton Island

# WALLASEA ISLAND

*"It may not seem worth coming out so far to so little purpose, but Wallasea, a true island between the Crouch and the Roach, is so characteristic of one kind of Essex that it should not be missed, even though the road goes no further and no public paths cross the watery flats."*

MARCUS CROUCH, *Essex*

Wallasea is the second largest of the six islands in the Essex Archipelago and, apart from Foulness, is probably the most full of activity, possessing its own farm, timber yard and wharf, yachting marina, caravan site and public house. The only one to the north of the Roach, the island is the most easily accessible of the six as it is open to the public and no permission is required to visit it.

It has been argued that Wallasea is not really an island at all since, except at times of extreme high tide, it is possible to drive straight onto the island without the slightest fear of getting wet. The Rochford Hundred historian, Philip Benton, writing in 1867, records that even then "Wallasea was formerly an island but is now joined to the mainland by a causeway", so the permanent connection to the mainland has clearly been firmly established for well over a century. Maps of former days, however, produced before the road was made up, clearly show that Wallasea was indeed a distinctly separate area of land from the mainland. Wallasea is actually a very large island - just under four miles in length by a little over a mile wide at its greatest extent - but it does not appear this big to the casual visitor as all the activity on it is concentrated in a small area in the north-western corner and the entire extensive remainder is given over exclusively to farmland. Here, the land stretches endlessly eastward until it seems to merge imperceptibly with the sea and the sky. This endless, flat and open land is similar in many ways to that of neighbouring Foulness Island though the wildlife population on Wallasea is not quite as varied, despite its protection from all but the boots of farmworkers and the most ambitious of ramblers.

The name 'Wallasea' derives directly from the words "wall" and "sea" - a seawall having been built round the island many centuries ago to protect its valuable agricultural land just as at other places around the county's coast. According to Rochford District Council (its administrative district) the earliest known historical reference to Wallasea dates from 1229, when it was known as 'Walfliet', the former name of the estuary created by the merging of the Rivers Roach and Crouch which pass either side of the island. The presence of three 'Red Hills', however, gives evidence that the island was known to the Romans a long time before that (the reddish earthen mounds being all that is left of their once profitable salt-making industry).

Wallasea has certainly had more than its fair share of name changes over the years, later names after Walfliet including 'Walset' (1309), 'Walet' or 'Walfletys' (1534), 'Wallettys' or 'Watys' (1540), 'Wallets' (1557), 'Wallett' or 'Wallfleet' (1594) and 'Wallot' Island (1678). The variety of names in use may partly be explained by the fact that the island was, in a similar way to Foulness and Canvey Islands, originally divided up into the ownership of five mainland parishes - Canewdon, Eastwood, Paglesham, Great Stambridge and Little Wakering - whose principal landowners were keen to expand their agricultural holdings by taking over the fertile marshland of the adjacent island. Curiously, however, the modern name for the island's sole remaining farm, Grapnells, is thought to derive from the family of Grapinel who held land further afield in Prittlewell in 1086 at the time of the Domesday survey.

Wallasea was once home to seven farms, spanning between them over 2,000 acres, but only Grapnells has survived. The adjacent oyster fisheries, dating from Roman times, have had their own share of suffering, being severely damaged during the Great Tide in 1953 and the intensely cold winter a decade later, and have never managed to recover to their full potential. Benton described them at their height as "a property of great value [which] under recent assessment have been doubled and quadrupled: these oysters have been celebrated for centuries as the best in England". During the Second World War the oysters off Wallasea Island were consumed in great numbers by soldiers who were stationed in the area - surely a special treat away from the standard wartime rations!

Other important industries at Wallasea which have grown up over more recent years include boat building and the thriving timber yards, which were established there in 1928 to handle the bulk importation of timber from the Baltic region. The deep water berths off the island proved ideal for the construction and launch of large numbers of naval patrol and assault craft during the Second World War, while the importance of the island's wharves, in existence long before their use for Baltic timber importations, had already been recognised over a century earlier by a proposal in 1811 for the construction of a railway to London, one of the earliest known railway plans of its kind. This, it was presumably thought by the scheme's backers at the time, would enable goods off-loaded at the wharves to be transported to the Capital as quickly as possible. Needless to say, the proposal never got off the ground.

Today Wallasea is the home of the Essex Marina which, together with the yachting interest at Burnham on the other side of the River Crouch, makes the area one of the most active for sailors in the county, some of the berths here being capable of taking craft to a depth of 33 feet. Boat building still continues as it has done since those extremely productive days of the Second World War and the island plays host to numerous chandlers and other marine-related retailers. These days the only commercial shipping activity to be seen in the Crouch, once an extremely busy working river, is that of the timber ships coming to Baltic Wharf from the continent. During the 1980s over 100,000 tons of timber was off-loaded there each year.

An ancient ferry service from Wallasea to Burnham has recently been reinstated in the summer months, following the success of a trial venture for the 1993 East Coast Boat Show (held in Burnham). Pleasure trips are also now laid on from Wallasea, upriver to Battlesbridge and downriver out into the estuary to see seals basking on the mudflats. Other old ferry routes to Foulness and Creeksea (the latter commemorated in the name of the island's only inn and in existence as long ago as 1625) have not, however, yet been re-established.

Essex Marina at Wallasea is the best equipped in the area and provides many basic facilities. The *Wardroom* hotel was specially built in 1966 to cater for the needs of visiting yachtsmen, though it has since had something of a chequered history. On the water itself boats can be chartered locally and fishing trips are often laid on.

Life on the island has not, however, always been wonderful. Serious flooding has been as prevalent here as elsewhere around the Essex coast. In 1736, for example, it was reported that "Peart of Wallis lland is now under water every flood tyde". In November, 1897, following the 'Black Monday' inundation, up to three quarters of the island was said to be under water. During the Great Tide of 1953, some four centuries after the first flooding of the island was recorded, the whole area of the Essex Archipelago was under water, the low-lying land and surrounding creeks being separately indistinguishable from each other for miles around. At Wallasea itself several inhabitants were forced to spend the night in a hayloft because they had no hope of getting off the island since the floodwater had covered the access road to the mainland and was up and over the walls by the time it was realised that something was seriously wrong. The landlady of the *Creeksea Ferry Inn* and her three remaining customers were similarly forced to seek refuge in the upper storey of the hostelry as a brave but vain attempt to drive to safety through the floodwater had to be abandoned.

The problem at Wallasea was that the seawalls held so well that no-one who was left on the island realised that there was anything wrong until it was too late. By the time the water began to spill over the top of the seawall, there was nothing that could be done to get off the island and it simply "filled like a dish in minutes". The whole island was soon under a flat sheet of water, five or six feet deep. Thirty-seven human beings were on Wallasea when the water broke in, along with countless farm animals which were forced to take refuge where the water was lowest - in the not exactly ideal and extremely exposed position on top of the seawall.

A police patrol had been unable to assess the situation accurately during the hours of darkness, believing it not to be too bad, but daylight told a different story. A haystack had been moved from one end of island to the other, whilst boats tied up at the landing stage and wood from the timber yard had been carried off by the floodwater and were now floating about all over the island. Gaps began to appear in the seawalls, which had largely held firm during the initial inundation, and more water poured in with every subsequent tide. Two people died on Wallasea - one of the customers of the *Creeksea Ferry Inn* who had been trapped downstairs by the first onrush of water and the island's postman who had been reported missing at the outset, but whose body was not discovered until a week later. All but six of the people trapped on the island were taken off by boat the following day, the six in question being members of the farming family living on the comparatively high land at Grapnells Farm who chose to stay behind to look after their animals. The last cattle in the whole county to be evacuated from flooded areas in the aftermath of the Great Tide turned out to be the dairy cows from Grapnells Farm.

When the waters eventually receded it could be seen that the east and south walls of the island had been almost completely demolished and timber stocks valued at more than a quarter of a million pounds were scattered all over the island. A plan was drawn up to construct a huge sandbag dam north-to-south across the middle of the island, cutting it completely in half in order to try to contain the floating timber in the western end and effectively to abandon the severely damaged eastern end of the island to the sea. The dividing wall, 800 yards long, four-and-a-half feet wide and a similar distance in height, was erected within three weeks of the inundation by 400 men who took barely a week to complete the job. The eastern end of the island and a part of nearby Havengore Island were amongst the last places in the county to be cleared of floodwater, but the land cordoned off was not indefinitely returned to the sea and was later reclaimed.

'The Creeksea Ferry Inn', Wallasea Island

Essex Marina, Wallasea Island

'The Wardroom', Wallasea Island

On Monday, 2nd February, 1953, BBC radio reporter, Charles Garner, flew over the island and relayed to his horror-struck audience details of what he had seen. "The familiar curve of East Anglia, the estuaries, the Thames mouth islands, firm enough lines in your school atlas, now have no boundaries but are at the will of the sea," he told them. "You've got to see roofs sticking out of the water to realise this isn't a pretty bit of scenery, but it's the end of people's homes, the end of their way of living, and in many cases the end of their lives."

Even when it was over, no residents were allowed to return to Wallasea for almost two months. The River Board, which had been responsible for supervising many aspects of the clean-up operation, had advised the clerk of Rochford Council with regard to both Wallasea Island and neighbouring Potton Island that there should be "no question of a return of residents to these islands until work has been carried out to the walls which will make them reasonably secure against high tides and storms".

Thirty years after the Great Tide Wallasea was one of the areas which was particularly badly hit by the 1987 'hurricane', perhaps the most talked about freak weather phenomenon in recent years. A landing stage at the Essex Marina, complete with 60 boats still attached to it, broke free from its foundations and was blown north across the River Crouch towards Burnham. Many of the smaller boats were either severely damaged or totally destroyed.

The population of Wallasea Island has always been small. In mid-Victorian times it was recorded that there were 13 houses and 135 inhabitants, though the population in the summer could rise dramatically, sometimes to as much as 300. One of the principal drawbacks of living on the island at this time, as with many other coastal places and islands in the county, was the absence of a reliable supply of fresh drinking water. Philip Morant, writing in 1768, puts it bluntly by remarking that "the water of this place is not fit for the kitchen"! This problem was eventually resolved by the introduction of a number of Artesian wells which in turn led directly to a noticeable long-term improvement in the health of the island's inhabitants.

Unlike neighbouring Foulness Island, Wallasea has never had its own church, so churchgoers have always had to leave the island if wanting to visit a place of worship. This appears to have been something of a bone of contention with islanders since it was recorded during the last century that no-one had ever visited the island "for spiritual purposes" and the Bishop of Rochester was asked to see if a vicar could be provided. The island's inhabitants were ultimately visited by the incumbents from nearby Paglesham and Eastwood but these visits tended to be sporadic so that, particularly in the winter, when no-one seemed too keen to venture out to such a remote place, islanders were "left to their own guidance".

Although there was no church on Wallasea, the island did once have its own school, allegedly the smallest in the country, which was certainly operational towards the end of the last century. Unfortunately, however, it had something of a chequered history and closed down within twenty years of opening, its pupils being transferred to a larger school elsewhere. A 1906 Press report describes the island as deserted and the school and other buildings as occupied by mice and birds. One man and one boy looked after all the livestock on the island at this time and the labouring population had seriously declined from the hundred or so men of former times, many of them members of travelling gangs of Irish labourers, to just eight. The school was actually reopened in the years leading up to the First World War, some of its pupils travelling across the water from Foulness Island because the route to the Wallasea school was easier for them to complete than that to the Foulness school. The establishment actually stayed in business a little longer on this occasion, lasting until the early 1940s when, to quote Mr. Jackson of the Essex Education Committee, "it ceased to exist soon after fifty percent of the pupils left, that is the headmistress, wife of the local foreman, moved, and took her two children with her". The building itself held on until being destroyed by the 1953 floods, after which it was sold on for development.

The decline in school attendance was not helped by the agricultural depression in the 1930s when almost the entire island was allowed to revert to rough pasture and was used for the keeping of cattle and sheep, as the more labour-intensive arable use was not as profitable as it had been. Virtually all the island's infrastructure was allowed to deteriorate as the population dropped and the farming industry, which for many of them had been a way of life, could no longer support them.

With the arrival of the Second World War Wallasea saw a surprising amount of action, undoubtedly because of its proximity to the River Thames (a major navigational aid for London-bound German bombers) and to the government base on Foulness Island, and it was said to have been the most severely affected of all the county's smaller islands. As early as 1940 the island's seawall was damaged by three bombs which landed just to the east of a building known as Tile Barn, whilst the following year 11 devices exploded at Grass Farm and another two caused damage to a bungalow and outbuildings at Lower Barn Farm. In 1942 a young farmworker was taken to nearby Rochford Hospital for treatment after handling a recently-landed shell, whilst two haystacks went up in flames in separate bombing incidents at Old Pool and Grass Farms, the first of a large number of direct hits to Wallasea in a matter of days. The attacks continued even into 1945 when long-range missiles exploded at Grapnells and Tile Barn Farms causing some damage to buildings.

The onset of war had caused all pleasure-craft boat building on the island to be ceased as the Wallasea Bay Yacht Station Ltd. (as the Essex Marina was formerly called) began to undertake repairs for the Admiralty. This relationship proved to be so successful that the company later built several 115-feet long motor torpedo boats for them and the seawall had to be specially adapted to enable the first of these vessels to be launched. After the war, the firm's expertise was recognised by the Admiralty with congratulations that it had been the fastest company in England to build such a boat.

Tile Barn, mentioned above, was also known as the Devil's House, as a number of curious incidents are alleged to have occurred there. Some guests who were staying there on one occasion claimed to have been thrown out of bed during the night, the sound of wings beating could be heard in some rooms and one room in particular often became intensely cold all of a sudden for no apparent reason. A sighting of the Devil is actually claimed to have been made on the marshes near Tile Barn and the house was reputed to be haunted by the ghost of a witch's familiar, a small animal or spirit which the witch could control, which in this case took the form of an ape. One night in 1938 a herd of cattle inexplicably charged the stockyard gates and knocked them flat and galloped wildly all over the marshes. 'Old Mother Redcap', the Foulness and Wallasea witch, was also active in the area, reputedly seen crossing the sky on a hurdle at night. Some claim that the origin of all these 'things that go bump in the night' stories was the extravagantly reported escapades of a young bullock escaping from its pen and finding its way into the house and up the wide staircase into a bedroom, but the building was once in the ownership of one Sir Thomas Davall, whose name could easily have been corrupted by the rough local dialect to form the name 'Devil's House'. One-time farm labourer, Albert Martin, told James Wentworth Day in the 1940s that Devil's House, which has now been demolished, was an old thatched place with a great old barn and it was very lonely and foreboding. The old building is actually shown as "Devil's House" on the 1777 map of John Chapman and Peter André.

Today the principal attractions of Wallasea Island to the outsider are the Essex Yacht Marina and the *Creeksea Ferry Inn*, one of those lovely old pubs 'out in the country' where one can go for a peaceful evening drink or lunchtime meal to avoid all the clamour of nearby Southend.

On the mainland next to the island is the Lion Creek Nature Reserve, owned and managed by the Essex Wildlife Trust (EWT). It comprises a 14-acre natural salt lagoon, edged by public footpaths, and includes many rare species of plant, animal and bird life, including Roesel's bush cricket and the adder. A specially erected hide enhances the reserve's wildlife viewing potential. After a busy history, peace and quiet is what Wallasea Island has to offer most people today.

Wallasea Island ferry trips

## THE CROUCH & BLACKWATER GROUP

The Crouch & Blackwater Group of islands is really the River Blackwater group with the addition of Bridgemarsh Island in the River Crouch. Bridgemarsh is a curious island - a raised area of marshland in a wide part of the river, now virtually lost to the sea following neglect of its seawalls.

The islands in the River Blackwater are also an unusual grouping, as they differ quite widely despite being in the same river. Pewet Island, near the mouth of the river, is a long, narrow raised area of marshland which shields the entrance to Bradwell Marina. Ramsey Island, further upriver, is now joined imperceptibly to the mainland, following land reclamation and the blocking of Ramsey Creek. Only Osea and Northey Islands - two of Essex's handful of 'proper' islands - can really be considered in anyway similar, partly from their size, partly from their positions in the middle of the river and partly from their proximity to each other.

Of the five groups of islands covered in this book, this is perhaps the most diverse. It is also the only group whose islands lie deep within the county's rivers - Northey and Osea in particular are true river islands, not fragments of broken off coastline like the majority of Essex islands.

Bradwell Marina, with Pewet Island in the background

# BRIDGEMARSH ISLAND

*"An object lesson to those who may be tempted to neglect the sea defences."*
MARCUS CROUCH, *Essex*

Bridgemarsh Island lies in the Easter Reach of the River Crouch, about three miles up-river from the yachting centre at Burnham, and is best approached by land from the village of Althorne, on the southern edge of the Dengie Hundred. It is the only proper island in the whole of the Crouch outside the Essex Archipelago at the river's mouth.

Originally a complete island, encircled for protection against the sea by walls and embankments, it is today visible only in parts above the water at high tide since, due to neglect, it was once irretrievably flooded and the majority of the valuable agricultural marshland which it comprised was eternally lost.

As recently as the 1930s the island was still protected by seawalls and offered valuable pasture for cattle and sheep and shelter in its internal dykes and fleets for all kinds of creatures, particularly wild duck and eels. An old ruined cottage, presumably once used by the farmhands responsible for looking after the sheep and cattle, stood at the western end of the island at this time, the chimney of which was home to a pair of peregrine falcons which returned annually to their nesting site despite the noisy and obtrusive (and extremely popular) use of the island for the hunting of wildfowl.

By the end of the 1940s, however, following a day of strong easterly gales which whipped up an exceptionally high tide, the seawall, whose upkeep had been foolishly neglected, had been completely demolished and the low-lying marshland island had been reclaimed by the sea. Many sheep were lost in the inundation and the fine crops and vast hauls of eels which were once to be had there were sadly to be no more. As with many other Essex coastal areas there is actually a long history of farming and flooding hereabouts and the earlier floods of 1736 which devastated much of south-eastern England claimed the lives of almost 300 sheep on Bridgemarsh Island.

Forty years later, Bridgemarsh was shown as a marshy island enclosed by a seawall on Chapman and André's map of 1777 and, like so many of the county's islands, is still little more than marshland today. The island had been drained, piled and enclosed a decade before Chapman and André's survey, presumably in response to the floods of 1736, and it was already being used for the cultivation of tall grasses. This was apparently proving to be quite successful, since the island was assessed for rating purposes by about 1768.

Even so, due to neglect and argument about whether the land owner or the local authorities were responsible for the upkeep of the seawalls, the island continued to be flooded from time to time, suffering particularly badly in the 'Black Monday' floods of November, 1897, when yet more livestock and this time some of the land were lost forever. Floods occurred again in 1928, after which the Chelmsford-based *Essex Chronicle* noted rather ironically that there was "no authority empowered to see that the walls were heightened as required" or to ensure that they were properly maintained.

By the time of the Great Tide in 1953, when the whole of the east coast suffered serious flooding, what was left of Bridgemarsh Island was not only being neglected but was actually actively 'vandalised' after the inundation during mainland seawall repair operations. Two hundred civilians and servicemen used what remained of the island's clay base to block seawall breaches on the banks of the River Crouch nearby. During the cleaning-up operation in February and March 1953, sandbags filled on Bridgemarsh Island were used to block what was to become the last remaining breach in the whole of the county's flood defences at nearby Norpits on the mainland. This was actually rather ironic, since before the clay extraction exercise the island had, for a time, been used as a site for a brick and tile works, fed by a tramway linking it to a quay on the river, which had been one of the earliest tramways to be used in the county.

The rapid development of saltmarsh inside the old seawall following the flooding has, however, led to Bridgemarsh Island becoming an important wildfowl area, owned for some time by a wildfowling society. The lack of care of the seawalls which led to the flooding, however, is a classic example of the ultimate cost of neglecting the sea defences: once-fertile farmland is now swamped irretrievably by sea water.

A century ago the island was approached by a ford across Bridgemarsh Creek, reached by a track from the main road alongside Stamfords Farm, but this disappeared long ago and the island these days is not quite so readily accessible, and neither is there quite so much to see. The best approach today is by water, either in the main channel of the River Crouch or from the private Bridgemarsh Marina which lies on the north bank of the river at the foot of the road serving Althorne railway station. The Bridgemarsh Island Cruising Club is also based in this location. Yachtsmen viewing the island should note that landing is not permitted, though those with boats of a shallow draught may well be able to navigate some of the creeks which now cut through the island.

Some remnants of the old seawalls remain and what is left of the island can be glimpsed at low tide. Some ruins from the old cottage which once stood on it can also be traced, whilst the lower part of the chimney which was once home to the peregrine falcons is itself still visible. Virtually all of the island is covered at times of high tide.

The origin of the name 'Bridgemarsh' is uncertain, though it seems likely that it comes from a former owner rather than from the juxtaposition of a bridge and a section of marshland, which at first glance might appear to be a more obvious derivation. Sixteenth century documents call it 'Brides Marsh' and 'Bredes Marsh', although the term 'Bridgemarsh' was in everyday use by the mid-18th century. There is still a Bridgemarsh Farm on the mainland nearby.

As for the future, the western end of Bridgemarsh Creek, which divides the island from the mainland, is beginning to silt up and it is thought that this action may well one day result in Bridgemarsh being joined permanently to the mainland.

Bridgemarsh Island from the mainland

## PEWET ISLAND

*"I landed on Peewit Island - and found no peewits there..".*
JAMES WENTWORTH DAY, *Coastal Adventure*

There are three islands in Essex which bear the name 'peewit' (or similar) - a result of their connection with the bird of that name, the peewit being a type of plover with a distinctive vocal call.  The first of these, on our geographical tour round the county from south to north, is to be found in the River Blackwater, just off the shore from Bradwell Waterside at the mouth of Bradwell Creek.  The Blackwater as a whole is now actively managed to balance the needs of visitors, local businesses and residents with the need to conserve wildlife and the natural environment.  Pewet (note the spelling) and the other islands in the river are all influenced by the provisions of this project.

Pewet Island is, in terms of physical appearance, a typical Essex island: low-lying, flat and marshy.  Used primarily in the past for wildfowling, it is a tranquil place today, providing shelter for the yachtsmen of Bradwell marina and lying a stone's throw from the waterside *Green Man*, often frequented by visitors to the nearby 7th century chapel of St Peter-on-the-Wall.  The nuclear power station looms up from the mainland barely a mile to the north-east, but the area manages to remain relatively undisturbed and surprisingly peaceful and quiet.  Had History chosen an alternative course, however, things could have been very different.

Just across the water, on the northern shore of the River Blackwater, lie the remains of the pier for the Tollesbury light railway, a short-lived scheme funded by the Great Eastern Railway (G.E.R.) for the dual purposes of 'exporting' fruit from the Tiptree fruit farms and of landing timber at Tollesbury and ferrying it quickly to London and East Anglia (via a connection to the main London-Norwich railway).

The project, however, was a disaster right from the start because, apart from anything else, the location of the landing facilities on the inside of the bend in the river at this point meant that sufficient water was not always available for ships to berth there (the pier at Tollesbury was specially constructed to try to improve this situation.) The scheme ran for only 14 years before being closed down.

Recent speculation that had the G.E.R. instead carried its Wickford to Burnham line an additional five miles beyond Southminster to Bradwell and had suitable berths been constructed in the mouth of Bradwell Creek, where the water was deeper for longer and where Pewet Island provided some shelter, the timber ships at least might well have been used to some degree of profitability. But how differently the area around Pewet Island might have looked!

It was not until the building of the nuclear power station in the area in the late 1950s and the construction of the yacht marina at around the same time that the full potential of the creek and the usefulness to which the island could be put was fully realised. The modern marina of today is one of the most impressive in the county and, with the Blackwater being a busy recreational river, a pleasant afternoon's boat-watching can easily be had there. In fact, the related maritime sign - "Dead Slow: No Wash" - is the only man-made thing of note on Pewet Island! On the nature front, seagulls and wading birds are amongst the many feathered visitors. The saltmarsh on the island, which is often covered during high spring tides, is an important natural habitat in the area.

Though situated in the Dengie Hundred, a relatively remote part of the county, Bradwell Waterside was historically comparatively easy to access by water from both the sea and from such places as Mersea Island (see later) which are visible from the seawall. There is a nice atmosphere here which Pewet Island is very much a part of - and the area is well worth a visit.

The remains of Tollesbury Light Railway pier, looking across to Pewet Island

# RAMSEY ISLAND

*"the... enclosed meadows ... known as Ramsey Island..."*
HARVEY BENHAM, *The Last Stronghold of Sail*

Thanks largely to improved sea defences, Ramsey Island, in St Lawrence Bay on the southern shore of the River Blackwater, three miles south-west of Pewet Island, is now no longer a genuine island at all. The large lake to the west of the current population centre on the western shore of the bay and the numerous ditches and channels which reach out from it across the meadowland of Ramsey Marsh give some indication of the degree to which the 'island' used to be separated from the mainland, but, as a result of the combined effect of a series of land reclamations which began in the latter half of the 10th century and the blocking up of Ramsey Creek, there is no such separation evident there today. Only at times of severe flood, such as during the 1953 'Great Tide', does Ramsey now return to its former island status.

Though still today largely undeveloped, the area around Ramsey Island was certainly known as long ago as the Roman period as the presence of a so-called 'Red Hill' there provides what is thought to be evidence of early salt production facilities such as can be found at many other sites around the Essex coast. Dr. P. H. Reaney records that the name is derived from the land's designation as the "island and marsh of 'Hraefning'", itself derived from an Old English personal name, perhaps belonging to a one-time landowner of the island.

Despite the predominantly rural nature of the area, some development has taken place: since Victorian times the old village of Ramsey has developed from just a handful of weatherboarded cottages into a sizeable holiday centre, stretching from the western shores of St Lawrence Bay round the promontory of The Stone towards the parish of Steeple, in which half the island lies (the other half lies in the parish of St Lawrence).

Since World War II a caravan park and marina have been developed at Ramsey as the holiday trade there has continued to grow and St Lawrence Bay has become a popular venue for a wide range of watersports, such as water-skiing, jet-skiing and windsurfing. The growing popularity of the place has, however, brought with it some problems.

Ever since the beginnings of expansion in the early 1960s, the growing tourist industry there led to a large influx of weekend holidaymakers descending on the village throughout the summer months. This resulted in a considerable increase in the demand for fresh drinking water and, partly because of the need to provide for this, a new water main was taken from the county's central Danbury trunk supply at Runsell Green to a specially-erected water tower at Cold Norton and water was pumped from there to Ramsey via, initially, a water tower at Latchingdon and then, by 1966, to a new tower on the hill by the church at St Lawrence. This St Lawrence water tower is now one of the major landmarks in the area.

Today, Ramsey Island is still a popular recreational area, providing marine-related attractions for visitors and the proverbial shop and public house for permanent 'island' residents. The area is administered by its own St Lawrence Bay parish council and it is part of the River Blackwater Site of Special Scientific Interest (SSSI).

Yachts at Ramsey Island

## OSEA ISLAND

*"I sailed to Osea Island - that pleasant Danish name - and found only a farm and a home for inebriates."*

JAMES WENTWORTH DAY, *Coastal Adventure*

The next island upriver in the Blackwater from Ramsey Island is Osea Island. This, and its near neighbour, Northey Island, are two 'proper islands' - mid-stream, of a good size, inhabited and with plenty of interest on them.

Dr. P. H. Reaney suggests that the island's name derives ultimately from its description as 'Ufe's island' - presumably Ufe was once a landowner there. The present name has been variously recorded elsewhere as Oosy, Osey and Osyth Island, though no hint of an alternative derivation has been given.

The island appears to have been known to Man as long ago as Roman times since a site near the landward end of the long and winding access causeway which joins Osea to the mainland is thought to have been a major Roman pottery production centre, with many important archæological finds having been made there. The existence of a number of 'Red Hills' - believed to be the remnants of early salt-making facilities - which have been discovered both on the nearby mainland and on the island itself, provide further evidence of Roman occupation.

After the Romans had left, the history books are rather silent about the rôle which Osea played in the world and it is not until the Battle of Maldon in 991 which took place off nearby Northey Island (see the chapter on Northey for full details) that further mention is made of it, with the claim in contemporary documents that some of Earldorman Byrhtnoth's men who were killed by the Viking invaders were buried on the island.

A hundred years later, by which time the Normans had invaded and taken over the country, the island appears to have been quite a prosperous agricultural centre. The Domesday Book of 1086 records Osea as having a well-stocked fishery and enough pasture for 60 sheep.

After that nothing remarkable appears to have happened on Osea Island for a further 700 years, although presumably the agricultural successes continued throughout this time.

By the 18th century, however, the well-known author and traveller, Daniel Defoe, was able to write that the island was well-known to Londoners "for the infinite number of wildfowl - duck, mallard, teal and widgeon..." which it possessed. "They tell us," he recounts, "the island seems cover'd with them at

Charrington's inebriates' home and Seal Pond, Osea Island

'Village' centre, Osea Island

certain times of the year... and they go from London on purpose for the pleasure of shooting... but it must be remembered, too, that gentlemen who are such lovers of the sport, and go so far for it, often return with an Essex ague [fever] on their backs, which they find a heavier load than the fowls they have shot." The marshland fevers were clearly as prevalent on the smaller Essex islands such as Osea as they were on the larger islands of Canvey and Foulness (which, incidentally, Defoe also visited).

Even late into this century wildfowling was still a popular pastime on Osea but, according to the *Victoria County History*, "the bags now made will not compare with the sensational records handed down by tradition... Colonel Russell of Stubbers and his henchmen, 'Gabe' Clark and Amos Taylor, Linett of Bradwell, the Mussetts of Mersea and the Handleys and Hipseys of Maldon were the wildfowlers whose achievements are remembered...". The remnants of one or two decoy ponds, specially built by wildfowlers to attract and capture their prey, still remain from these times.

In Victorian times, Osea was secluded enough to find itself being used as the base for a remarkable institution - the "home for inebriates" referred to by James Wentworth Day in the quotation at the head of this chapter. Frederick Nicholas Charrington, a member of the famous brewery family, founded the home after apparently witnessing a drunken lout punching his (the drunk's) wife in the face outside one of the family's pubs because she had had the audacity to ask him for some money to provide their children with some food. Charrington later wrote of the incident that "it knocked her into the gutter and me out of the brewery". The £1 million that he subsequently realised from the sale of his brewery shares as a reaction to this shocking incident was largely spent on encouraging people to give up alcohol. The "house for gentlemen suffering from the baneful and insidious effects of alcohol" which he established on Osea Island was just one of the schemes he set up in an attempt to meet this goal.

A secluded self-contained island, surrounded for most of the day by water and with no public house to hand, would probably have seemed an ideal place to keep those suffering from a craving for alcohol away from the stuff and initially the scheme worked well. But, unfortunately for Charrington, local boat-owners soon began to wise up to the scheme and showed some commendable entrepreneurial flair by smuggling consignments of alcohol to the island's 'inmates' (hiding bottles under bushes under the cover of darkness) or by hiring boats out to enable the latter to row up-river to the inns and hostelries of Maldon where they could obtain their own intoxicating liquor without the need for any smuggling to take place. Charrington tried a variety of ideas to take his charges' minds off their drink, even setting up a small zoo with cockatoos, emus, kangaroos and seals on the island, but despite all his highly commendable efforts the fact that the drinkers themselves seemed to have no desire to abstain meant that the scheme was inevitably doomed to failure.

The same fate also confronted a plan to construct a defence battery on the island during the middle of the 19th century as part of a larger scheme to repair and upgrade the existing defensive fortifications which stood on Britain's southern and eastern coasts. Only later, in the early 1870s when the German Empire was growing on the other side of the water, were any actual steps taken to introduce improvements. Even then no battery was ever built on Osea as had been proposed.

The island did, however, later see considerable action at the hands of the Admiralty who used it as a secret base (designated HMS *Osea*) for construction and testing of coastal motor boats (CMBs) designed by Sir John Thorneycroft. Up to 1,000 self-supporting Navy personnel were crammed onto Osea during and for a short time after the First World War while these boats were being developed. They were very fast and were designed to move rapidly in on their targets, fire torpedoes at them and then get out again before being detected. They arrived a little too late to see much active service during the war, but they were employed successfully in Russia in 1919 where they destroyed some warships in Kronstadt harbour. There was also a railway on the island connected with this development activity and some of the rails can still be seen on the beach.

By the end of the Second World War (which had seen the construction of a pillbox at the eastern end of the island to watch out for enemy shipping entering the Blackwater) a completely different scheme was being put forward. This entailed the development of the island in the form of a holiday camp with beach huts, chalets, a dance hall, a cinema, several shops and even a crêche. Frederick Charrington had had similar plans several decades earlier, intending to build a row of mansions overlooking the river to the south of the island, but nothing had come of them.

Commercialism had boosted the economies of other Essex islands at this time (such as Canvey and Mersea) and it seemed that some thought the same could be done for Osea. But not all... "A pretty future for an island that is alight and alive with English history," wrote James Wentworth Day at the time. "You might as well put a holiday camp on Holy Island or start a funfair on

The causeway from Osea Island to the mainland

Old jetty, Osea Island

Runnymede. This threat must be countered and fought at all costs." Presumably it was costs of a different kind which meant that this ambitious project was never even started.

The island was for a long time used for study purposes by students from Cambridge University and access to it was by permission only. Access is still restricted, with two-thirds of the island now being owned by English Nature and the other third used for sheep farming. There are also a handful of permanent private residents, whilst the remainder of the dozen or so buildings that exist there are let out as holiday homes.

The sloping sandy beaches which the island possesses are just one of its many natural attractions (they were once very popular with tourists when access was unrestricted) and the peace, quiet and timeless feel of the 'village' (the biggest grouping of houses) have a tremendous appeal. Drinking water is provided by the island's own underground lake, whilst mains electricity has been laid on via a submarine cable from the mainland. There is a postal collection by van "subject to the tide", but the small general store that once existed has now closed down. The tidal causeway is the only real disadvantage of permanent island life on Osea - access to the mainland is totally dependant on the tides and consequently no household is complete without a tide table.

The waters around the island have always been a popular place to anchor for local yachtsmen as this is the nearest that a boat can be taken upstream towards Maldon and yet still remain floating at all states of the tide. The island has its own jetty on the southern side and another mooring area on the northern side. Barges bound for the industrial area at nearby Heybridge Basin on the mainland have often been seen unloading their cargoes to smaller craft in the waters around Osea. Many fossils have also been found on the beaches on the south side of the island.

There used to be a big post here sticking out of the water near the jetty which was known as 'the Barnacle' and which had initially been erected to enable the local agricultural machinery manufacturer, E. H. Bentall, to support his famous yacht *Jullanar* against it to allow the vessel's hull to be scrubbed clean of barnacles and other debris. The *Jullanar*, built in 1875, was such an important craft at the time that its design influenced that of racing yachts around the world throughout the next century.

Today, as well as the human population, Osea Island is used extensively by dark-bellied Brent Geese, which feed on grass in the fields there. Gulls, wading birds, pheasants and rabbits are also visible in abundance. The island was formerly home to a large number of elm trees before the Dutch Elm disease arrived to destroy them in the early 1970s.  A large heronry has also long since disappeared.

As the island is exclusively private land (along with the road that leads to it), permission must be sought for any intended visit there.  The mile-long causeway is crossable for only two hours either side of low tide, so car-drivers in particular should take care to check their tide tables!

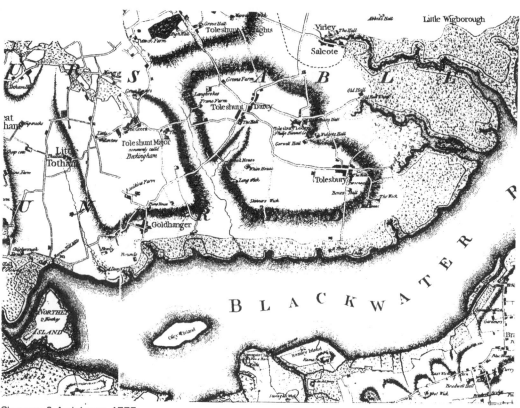

Chapman & André map, 1777

## NORTHEY ISLAND

*"From a Viking Invasion Base to a wildlife sanctuary."*
MALDON DISTRICT COUNCIL TOURIST PUBLICATION, *Northey Island*

To the west of Osea Island lies Northey Island, the other 'proper' (sizeable, mid-stream) island in the River Blackwater. Northey is the furthest island upstream in the river and can easily be seen from the ancient maritime town of Maldon on the mainland.

Northey, formerly known as Ruckholme or Hardholme Island (the word 'holm' translates as "river island"), is now a peaceful nature reserve, but it was once the site of one of England's greatest battles, where the English Earldorman Byrhtnoth lost his life in a valiant stand against an attempted Viking invasion.

The Battle of Maldon in 991 marked the beginning of the second great wave of Danish invasions to hit this country. A large fleet of Viking ships, under the command of their leader Anlaf (possibly, according to some sources, a corruption of the name for the famous Scandinavian king, Olaf Tryggvasson), crossed the North Sea from Denmark and began to carry out raids along the south east coast of England.

Having visited Sandwich, the country's principal port, and Ipswich, one of the largest local towns, they made their way up the Blackwater towards Maldon, an important strategic settlement which was then heavily fortified. The invaders were successfully forced back from the town and settled on Northey Island to gather themselves together.

Meanwhile, Maldon's townspeople called for reinforcements which arrived before the Vikings could attack again. These reinforcements were commanded by Earldorman Byrhtnoth, a strong and skilful fighter who, though by now in his sixties, was greatly respected by his fellow soldiers. One of the greatest landowners in the country at the time, Byrhtnoth is referred to in many contemporary documents from Essex to Cambridgeshire and his signature even appears on a number of significant deeds and agreements. A strong supporter of the King and the Church he was one of the most powerful men in England during this period.

Byrhtnoth's plan was to force the Vikings off the island and back into their ships, with the hope of making them sail away from the town, but when he arrived at Northey Island, which could be reached on foot only by a long narrow causeway, he discovered that the tide was in, covering the causeway, and that there was no way that the invading army could be engaged. While the two sides waited for the tide to go out the Vikings shouted their demands for money across the water, but Byrhtnoth would have none of it and just bided his time.

Eventually the tide began to go out and the Vikings began to attempt to cross the causeway. The route was so narrow, however, that the English forces, led by Wulfstan, Aldere (or Ælfhere) and Caccus (sometimes Maccus) managed to hold them at bay. Then, when they realised that their forces would not be able to reach the mainland and that the advantage lay clearly with the English forces, the Viking leaders began to claim that they should be allowed to cross to the mainland to enable a fair fight to ensue. Astonishingly, Byrhtnoth agreed to their request, perhaps with the intention of forcing a battle. The Viking forces were considerably larger than those of their opponents, but their full complement was still allowed to cross the causeway. Ultimately, and perhaps, in retrospect, predictably, the Vikings won the day.

Byrhtnoth was killed, along with the other leading English warriors, and his body was removed to Ely Abbey in Cambridgeshire for burial. Not all the body made it to Ely, however, as the Vikings cut off his head and took it away with them as a trophy so a wax ball was later made to take its place. But the Vikings had had something of a Pyrrhic victory. They had themselves lost many men and those that remained set sail without continuing inland, eventually retiring to another island base which they had set up at Sheppey in Kent. The English king, Ethelred, later paid them £10,000 to leave England, but having been once successful they of course returned to seek yet more fortune.

The Battle of Maldon marked the beginning of 25 years of successful Viking raids on England, culminating in 1016 at another Essex site, the village of Ashingdon, near Rochford, further south in the county, where Canute defeated a later English king, Edmund Ironside. It also marked the beginning of the first direct money tax on the English by the Vikings, which came to be known universally after this as 'Danegeld'. The whole event was commemorated at Maldon in 1991 by a locally-woven embroidery (similar to the Bayeux tapestry which depicts the Battle of Hastings) which is now housed in the 'Maeldune Centre' (the old St Peter's church).

Apart from the modern embroidery, the Battle of Maldon was also commemorated in a remarkable contemporary epic poem, apparently written by one of the survivors on the English side and comprising over 300 alliterative verses. This has become one of the most important early works in English literature and is the second oldest surviving Anglo-Saxon poem (after *Beowulf*). Unfortunately the original manuscript was lost in a fire in 1731 and not all of it has been passed down to us. A sizeable excerpt has survived, however, and various editions of this are now widely available from libraries and bookshops. A statue of Earldorman Byrhtnoth stands in a recess on the south wall of All Saints' church in Maldon High Street, itself an important historical treasure as it has a triangular tower unique in this country. It is recorded in some documents that Byrhtnoth's widow actually wove a tapestry of the battle shortly after it took place to commemorate his part in it, but none of this appears to have survived. The battlefield itself is, however, still relatively easy to identify as the landscape has changed very little there over the last 1,000 years and a visit to it can be quite an evocative experience.

The name of Northey Island is thought in some quarters to derive from the time of the Viking or Norsemen's invasion, though the authority on place names, Dr P. H. Reaney, attributes part of its name at least to the marshland surrounding the island. In the 12th century it was owned by the then all-powerful Beeleigh Abbey on the other side of Maldon but by the start of the 20 century Northey had found its way into private ownership. It was eventually sold in the 1920s to Sir Norman Angell, an MP who wanted a quiet place to continue his written work. An energetic man and a prolific author and journalist, Sir Norman became famous for his political books during the 1920s and 1930s and was awarded the Nobel Peace Prize in 1933 for his work in this field. At least one complete internationally acclaimed work, the 1938 publication *You and the Refugee*, was written on Northey.

Sir Norman's autobiography, *After All*, includes tales of many of his experiences while living on the island. He freely admits that his desire for somewhere as quiet and as peaceful as Northey was consciously felt. "This story," he writes, in a chapter devoted entirely to his time on the island, "is largely concerned with a boy's impulse to get away from a world which he felt to be cursed with problems it could not solve; to escape from contacts which only provoked misgivings, dismay and emotional frustration. Better the 'simple life of the open spaces'. Nearly everyone, I suppose, has this desire at times. The theory behind the move was that I would get away from the political world altogether."

It was Sir Norman who was responsible for modernising the island and its handful of buildings by establishing a mains water supply and introducing electricity and he also planted many trees and carried out long overdue repairs to the seawalls. He built the present three-storey Northey Island House in a strange and antiquated style, which gave a commanding view over all parts of the island and the approach to it over the tidal causeway from the mainland.

Sir Norman Angell's house, Northey Island

Entrance to Northey Island

He also established a none too profitable farming venture, often run in his absence by 'homesteaders' (usually a permanently resident married couple, helped by labourers).

The failure of Sir Norman's farming business was allegedly primarily due to the homesickness for the mainland which many of the female homesteaders felt - the island was, after all, cut off from civilisation for most of the day and communication with it was, as Sir Norman himself put it, "at times a serious economic obstacle". It could cause other problems, too. On one occasion, Sir Norman was sent a message from a female colleague saying that she "can sup with you after the theatre on Friday night". The message was delivered, however, as she "can *sleep* with you after the theatre on Friday night". The embarrassment caused to the respective parties was fortunately short-lived!

Sir Norman's first encounter with Northey was by complete accident, the island being 'discovered' during a sailing trip up the Blackwater. "Northey was a 'wrecked island'," he records of this time. "Originally its seawalls had enclosed about 300 acres of some of the best wheat land in England. But in the 19th century the seawalls had been breached and the agricultural depression forbade the cost of their restoration. What remained of the island available for farming was about 70 acres of high land well above high-water mark. There was a farmhouse on the place, and an enormous barn (both later to be destroyed by a bomb in the Second World War)."

There was also an old barge in the sale, which Sir Norman raised up out of the water and restored. Whilst on dry land the vessel was extremely popular with many of its owner's younger relatives and it became known affectionately as 'The Ark'. The remains of two barges can still be seen on the western side of the island, whilst a third lies hidden in the saltmarsh further into the centre.

Sir Norman bought the island from Vierville (or Vere) de Crespigny, a member of a much renowned local family who was known to be a little eccentric. It was rumoured that de Crespigny's family had helped their relative to buy the island in the first place because he would be out of the way and would thus cause them as little embarrassment as possible, but this move does not appear to have been too successful.

De Crespigny had a complex about Irish people, due to some past bad experience, and lived in constant fear of the island being invaded by them. He spent much of his time (including many nights) in a little hut built on wheels which could be moved around the island to strategic positions to enable him more effectively to see off any invaders. Trespassers, like the wildlife on Northey, were not immune from being shot at! When Sir Norman bought the island de Crespigny took a job as a game warden in Africa and was sadly, though not perhaps unexpectedly, trampled to death by an elephant whilst on one of his adventures.

But the venture of occupying Northey never realised the ambitions that Sir Norman had held for it. His success in escaping the troubles of the political world was replaced only by the troubles of the farming world - worries about swine fever, anthrax and maintaining adequate communication with the outside world. There was sometimes looting during his extended absences from the island and there were domestic disputes, too. "On one occasion," he recalls, "I arrived at the island to find the bailiff [the person running the farm in his absence] barricaded in the cottage, around which marched two discontented workmen with shotguns, loudly proclaiming their intention to 'do in' the people inside the cottage 'even if we swing for it'." This caused Sir Norman to remark ironically to his secretary: "It's evident we shall have to get back to London for a little peace and quiet"!

After the Second World War, Sir Norman gave the island to his nephew, Eric Angell Lane, who continued to improve the facilities on Northey, further repairing the seawalls and doing his best to farm the land. The vast majority of the original 300 acres could never be farmed, however, as it had long been lost to the saltings as a result of those early unrepaired breaches in the seawalls. A writer from the *Essex Naturalist*, touring the area as long ago as 1898, reported that Northey Island was rapidly reverting to salting. Serious flooding had occurred in 1707 and 1897 (when water lay on the island for over a year) and would later take place in 1901 and 1953. During the 'Black Monday' floods of November, 1897, the high tides breached the island's defences in a number of places and it was subsequently more or less abandoned due to the prohibitive cost of repairing the seawalls. Such a small exposed area, which was continually threatened by flooding, could never be farmed with any substantial profitability. In 1978 Mr Lane gave the island to the National Trust, along with neighbouring South House Farm on the mainland and the 200 agricultural acres which that possessed.

Northey today is still owned and managed by the National Trust and a Trust warden actually lives on the island. The large area of undisturbed saltmarsh which surrounds Northey is, like that at many other of the county's islands, a particularly important area for seabirds. The reserve's 260 acres, designated a Site of Special Scientific Interest (SSSI), is served by a specially laid nature trail and, though principally significant as a bird sanctuary, is home to a variety of interesting animal and plant species.

In recent years attempts have been made to improve the sea defences on the reserve - which is suffering some erosion - by using new methods of land reclamation. One idea - trialled here by the National Rivers Authority (now the Environment Agency) and since repeated successfully elsewhere - was that of "managed retreat", now called "coastal realignment". This involved the lowering of the existing seawall so that the sea could flood onto the island unchecked as far as an older seawall which lay some distance inland. This process allowed silt carried by the one-in-three high tides which flooded the island to be deposited on land and provide an area on which saltmarsh plants could become established. This new marshland area has consequently provided a firm base for plant growth and additional defence for the island from the sea.

Seabirds are particularly regular visitors to the reserve and during the winter Brent Geese especially are present in large numbers. Grass on the island is kept close mown to attract the geese and to try to dissuade them from landing on nearby mainland farmland where they can cause damage to crops by trampling them down. Over 2,000 geese were fed and protected on the special 'goose field' scheme on Northey in 1982 - the first time the scheme was tried - and they have been coming back in large numbers - 5,000 a year nowadays - ever since. Such 'wildfowl grazing' areas are actively encouraged in modern farming. There is also a bird hide on Northey to provide views of seabirds in the estuary.

Apart from the seabirds, short-eared owls are a common sight on the island, though the huge colony of ravens which once nested there in the 19th century has sadly long since disappeared. Access to Northey is still by the old Roman causeway over which the Vikings came, passable up to two hours either side of low tide, but - except during the annual September open day - permission is required from the Trust before visiting is allowed.

Cubs and brownies have in the past been given special permission to use the island for camping expeditions in the summer - a real teenage adventure story come to life. Sir Norman Angell, who had a great fondness for children, would surely have welcomed this enterprise.

Northey Island today remains a quiet 'out of the way' place, despite its proximity to the bustling town of Maldon and the wealth of marine activity which takes place in the vicinity. It is hard to imagine now that so peaceful an island once played such an important part in the history of English warfare.

# THE MERSEA GROUP

At the confluence of the Rivers Blackwater and Colne lies Mersea Island. This, and the large number of smaller surrounding marshland islands, are collectively covered here as 'the Mersea Group'.

Mersea itself is probably the most 'proper' island in the county. Unlike many of the others, it is not a broken-off fragment of low-lying marshland - it has decent altitude and was (before the road to it was built) completely separate from the mainland. It is the third largest island in the county (after Foulness and Canvey) and is substantially populated.

Around Mersea Island the smaller islands form into several groups. These can be found in Tollesbury Fleet and Salcott Channel (tributaries of the River Blackwater) to the south west; the Strood/Pyefleet Channel (which separates the island from the mainland) to the north and north west; Geedon Creek (a tributary of the River Colne) to the north; and Brightlingsea Creek (another Colne tributary) to the east.

The islands in this group have many similarities and interwoven histories. Sailing, smuggling and nature conservation are the recurrent themes of the Mersea Group.

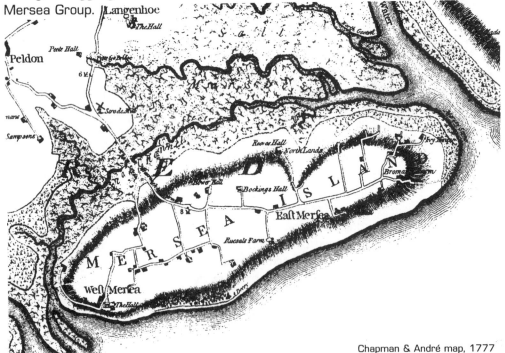

Chapman & André map, 1777

MERSEA ISLAND

*"Cross the Strood during the winter months after the temporary residents have left, when the wind from the North Sea is howling like a banshee and chilling every bone in one's body, when the torn clouds race angrily across the moon, then the mystery of the island wraps you in its magic embrace."*

GLYN MORGAN, *Secret Essex*

The third and last (on this geographical tour) of the large Essex islands is Mersea, an island quite unlike any other to be found around the county's shores. In a part of the country where islands, though present in great numbers, invariably comprise little more than low-lying marshland, Mersea is a pleasant surprise as it looms up out of the waters where the Rivers Blackwater and Colne converge, some five miles south of the old Roman town of Colchester. Even the most 'island-like' island in Essex, however, is connected to the mainland - in this case by a causeway, known as the Strood (pronounced 'Strode'), which supports the busy B1025 road.

Oval in shape and some four-and-a-half miles by two in size, Mersea Island is separated from the mainland by a narrow creek known as Pyefleet. The name 'Mersea' is thought to mean "island of the pool or mere", the pool being the area of water formed by the confluence of the estuaries of the Rivers Colne and Blackwater in which the island lies. The island rises to some 70 feet in height on a base of London Clay. The main east-west road runs along the top of this clay landscape and provides an excellent vantage point over the surrounding countryside to the north and seascape to the south. There is some marshland on the northern side of the island, generally protected by seawalls, but the southern shore has a mixture of low cliffs and long flat stretches of sand.

Administratively the island is divided into two distinct communities, known from their geographical positions as East and West Mersea, and it is the most easterly permanently inhabited island in Britain.

The two island settlements are very different. West Mersea is a built-up residential and commercial area, an active yachting and fishing centre and home to boat-builders, holiday camps, beach huts and traditional seaside attractions. Still relatively unknown to the outsider as recently as the 1920s, it was initially 'discovered' by visiting yachtsmen and marketed as a handy nearby seaside destination to the people of Colchester. It has now become an extremely popular tourist destination in the summer months. East Mersea, by contrast, is largely rural - predominantly agricultural, with houses dotted here and there and an extensive country park which borders on the important Colne Estuary National Nature Reserve (NNR). The island's population is just over 6,000, all but 300 of whom live in West Mersea.

Mersea's proximity to Colchester, an important Roman and Anglo-Saxon town, as well as its position on the east coast between two rivers has meant that over the centuries it has been one of the first stopping off places for invading armies, who invariably launched their attacks on the mainland from here and used the Colne and the Blackwater rivers to move their forces inland to attack the native strongholds of Colchester and Maldon. The Danes, for example, were here in 895, about the time they were at Canvey, when they were using the island as a base from which to launch an attack on London. It was so well placed geographically that they returned many times to set up temporary bases there. The famous failed attack on London in which King Alfred instructed his engineers to divert the River Lea and cause the Danish ships to be stranded without water was planned and initiated from Mersea.

A Romano-British burial mound, dating from the first century B.C., gives physical evidence of Roman occupation of Mersea long before the Vikings arrived. Excavation has revealed that the mound, 100 feet in diameter and over 20 feet high, contained a small internal chamber, 18 inches square and 21 inches high, whose walls were made of Roman tiles. Inside this chamber was a small square lead casket containing a glass bowl 11½ inches high, which itself contained the cremated remains of an adult. A British mound and a Roman burial seem a curious combination and many stories have circulated over the years in an attempt to explain this juxtaposition. Amongst these is the romantic notion that the excavated remains were those of the daughter of a Roman leader who fell in love with and married a British nobleman and who, when she died, was buried according to local custom. Sadly, there is no proof either way. The Mersea Mount or Barrow, as it has become known, can still be seen today, lying just to the north of the main road to East Mersea near Barrow Hill Farm.

Elsewhere on the island an unusual 'Wheel Tomb' is also thought to date from Roman times, since examples of similar positively identified constructions have been found in other places throughout the old Roman Empire. In a garden in Beach Road, 200 yards east of West Mersea parish church, the 'tomb', which is 65 feet in diameter, consists of a small hexagonal room connected to a larger encircling wall by six other straight walls and when viewed from above it resembles a spoked wheel. Claims have been made that the structure is not actually a tomb at all but the base of an old Roman lighthouse, erected on the site to guide shipping into the Colne and Blackwater estuaries. Support for this theory includes the fact that the structure is situated quite close to Pharos Lane - 'Pharos' was Greek for lighthouse, a name taken from the island on which stood the first known lighthouse (one of the Seven Ancient Wonders of the World).

Traces of Roman villas and mosaic pavements have also been found on the island, mostly in the vicinity of West Mersea parish church, and over 25 Red Hills, the remnants of ancient salt-making facilities which are to be found at many coastal sites around the county, have also been positively identified. Some even earlier occupation has also been recorded with finds of Neolithic axes and a Bronze Age beaker and flint dagger. The bones of a mammoth, removed to Colchester museum, have also been discovered on Mersea.

Apart from the remnants of salt-making facilities, the Romans left behind another important industrial occupation, that of oyster farming, which continues in the Colne estuary to this day. In the 10th century hundreds of men and boys were involved in oyster cultivation hereabouts, specifically the cultivation of the so-called 'West Mersea Native' oyster. This long association with oysters is commemorated annually in October by a great oyster feast, with celebrations being led by the Mayor and other Colchester dignitaries. Attendance is by invitation only. There is a ballot for tickets for the few remaining places (usually over-subscribed!). Colchester Borough Council tourist information literature acknowledges the importance of this industry, stating that the Pyefleet Channel is "the historic breeding ground of the Colchester oysters".

The Strood causeway, which crosses the Pyefleet Channel, is a further reminder of the island's Roman history since it was initially established by the Romans during their occupation of Colchester to provide a safe route across to an island which was used extensively by them for recreation and as a site for recuperation after illness. Many 'old soldiers' were retired to Mersea after their tour of duty was over. The 18th century author, Philip Morant, also believed that it was home to a Roman General, possibly even the so-called Count of the Saxon Shore, whose responsibility it was to oversee the east coast defences and to ensure that they were always ready to repel any Saxon invasion.

Both the island's two parish churches bear closer inspection from an historical perspective. The church of St Peter and St Paul at West Mersea stands on the site of a Roman building and contains both Roman and Anglo-Saxon features. Only three miles away, across the mouth of the River

Blackwater to the south-west, St Cedd founded the first Christian chapel in the county at St Peter-on-the-Wall, Bradwell, in 654 A.D. and it is believed that he may also have visited West Mersea, whose church also features a dedication to St Peter. It is said that in Roman times, when the sea level was somewhat lower than today, it was even possible to cross the Blackwater estuary on horseback from Bradwell to Mersea. If this is true, the route would surely also have been in existence in Cedd's time. It is further recorded that a route marked by posts similar to those marking the extent of the allegedly Roman Broomway at Foulness (see earlier chapter) was seen in this area during an exceptionally low tide in 1906. Were these the boundary markers for a Roman road to Bradwell? A Roman building which stood to the east of the present church within the present churchyard is thought to have been founded around St Cedd's time in the seventh century. The same site may also have supported a collegiate minster (a church serving a wider area) in the 10th century - wills of the Saxon earldorman, Aelfgar, and his daughters Aethelflaed and Aelfflaed, make reference to such a building. As for the structure of the present building, the lower parts of the west tower are predominantly early Norman, though Roman bricks are incorporated into the design. The later tower is supported by 14th century buttresses, while the rest of the church is late Mediæval. The height of the nave was increased during an expansion project in 1833 and some wall paintings were also introduced in the 19th century. To the east of the church stands West Mersea Hall, which itself dates from the 18th century, though an old abbey or priory which once stood nearby and which may have had connections with the collegiate minster has long since disappeared.

The church of St Edmund King & Martyr at East Mersea is best known for its associations with the writer Sabine Baring-Gould, rector there in late Victorian times (1871-81). His autobiographical publications, *Ten Years On The Mud* and *Early Reminiscences*, both recall his time at East Mersea, whilst his novel *Mehalah* is set on and around the island and is based on characters who lived there during his day. The hymn Now The Day Is Over was also written by Baring-Gould, who was a prolific author, reputedly to be chimed on the bells of the church, whilst he is probably best remembered now for another hymn, Onward Christian Soldiers. The building itself has seen little change since Baring-Gould was there. It is nearly all 15th century with a big Perpendicular west tower supported by diagonal buttresses and including features such as battlements and a higher stair turret. In the churchyard is a rare iron-bound grave of a 15-year-old girl, dating from 1848. Inside the church is one of the county's best examples of a pulpit with a tester (sounding board), together with

St Edmund, East Mersea

Crumbling cliffs at Cudmore Grove Country Park, East Mersea

some 16th and 17th century tombstones. During the Civil War the church suffered some damage at the hands of Cromwell's soldiers who camped inside it and removed the rood screen and stained glass windows, whilst its then rector, Israel Edwards, was expelled from his living (he was later restored). Less damage resulted when the building was garrisoned during subsequent campaigns when a united English force was preparing to repel both Dutch and French invasions. The church's Saxon dedication implies that there may once have been a building of that period on the site.

The island was quite an important strategic location during the Civil War, specifically in respect to the Siege of Colchester in 1648 when supporters of the Royalist army which was trapped inside that town's walls by Parliamentarian forces outside them launched an abortive attempt to reach their companions by sailing up the River Colne where they believed they could not be seen by their opponents. Unfortunately for the Royalists, however, the Parliamentarians had ships of their own hidden in Brightlingsea Creek, a tributary of the Colne, and attacked them as they progressed up-river. The capture by the Parliamentarians of an old fort on Mersea Island which provided a good vantage point over the surrounding waters meant that all Royalist shipping movements could be monitored and any attempts to relieve those trapped in the town could be immediately thwarted.

Mersea Island has always had close links with the sea and even before the Civil War period there was a great deal of shipping activity in the area. In mediæval times the island provided a ship for Sir Walter de Manny's expedition to Brittany in 1342, during the Hundred Years' War, to relieve the Countess of Hennebon from the attacks of Charles de Blois, whose claim to the Duchy of Brittany, which she stood in the way of, was supported by France.

The area at the western end of the island where most of the present marine activity is concentrated is actually known as 'The City', though it is in reality no more than a grouping of old wooden cottages, boat yards and jetties.

Many years prior to the Civil War both Henry VII and Henry VIII had been responsible for improving Britain's defences and the fort at Mersea which the Parliamentarians occupied had been specifically introduced to protect access to the River Colne from foreign invasion. Built in 1543 at a cost of just under £400, it comprised a fortified earthwork and triangular blockhouse, each side of which was some 300 feet long. Semi-circular bastions were provided at the three corners, each armed with 12 guns a piece. The fort was operational for barely a decade when its cannons were taken out of service and sent to the Tower of London. Although revived and re-armed during the reign of Elizabeth, presumably in preparation for the expected Spanish invasion attempt, it soon fell into disrepair once more. Clearly, though, this structure, or at least a descendant of it, was operational again by the time of the Civil War. The Mersea Stone, at the eastern end of the island on the banks of the Colne, and other minor remains elsewhere are now all that is left of these early defensive installations.

In the early 1800s a new chain of sea defences was provided all along the coastline and revised fortifications were introduced both at the eastern end of the island, to guard the river, and on the landward side, to cover the Strood. Barges carrying four guns each were additionally located at the mouths of the Rivers Colne and Blackwater. These defences did not see any action, however, as the anticipated Napoleonic invasion never materialised.

A look at later 19th century Mersea is probably best provided by the prolific pen of Baring-Gould, though his views of the place are coloured by the fact that he did not particularly enjoy his time there as a learned clergymen amongst "ignorant" fishermen and farmers. One principal island occupation at this time was wildfowling, the indulgence of which, the parson recalls in his *Early Reminiscences*, was a contributory factor to the ill health of many of the island's population. Much as at Canvey and Foulness, people spending too much time in the marshes went down with agues (fevers) and rheumatism. "My impression was that generations afflicted with these complaints acquired in the marshes had lowered the physique and mental development of the islanders," Baring-Gould recalls superciliously.

Certainly the island's inhabitants depended on the surrounding waters for their livelihood. "An industry exercised by the women and children of West Mersea," Baring-Gould writes elsewhere, "was the collecting of winkles off the flats for the London market. In order for them to be able to walk on the wet clay they wore flat boards cut into ovals under their soles and braced tightly over the instep and about the ankles. Walking or gliding about on these, they stooped to collect the molluscs into a basket held in the left hand. Woe to such as slipped and fell. The adhesive clay held him or her fast by the arms."

On the south side of the island, seaward of East Mersea church, a channel was excavated and a landing stage built so that barges bringing coal and 'London muck' to the island could easily berth and off-load their cargoes as close as possible to their intended destination. 'London muck' - exactly what it sounds like - was used as a manure for the fields on Mersea until it was replaced by the spreading of sprats, locally caught no doubt! Gulls arrived in their numbers to relieve the farmers of this latter dressing and small boys were employed to scare them away. "The smell," records Baring-Gould, whose rectory was close to East Mersea church, "was not enjoyable, but the odour was superior to London muck." The empty barges which had off-loaded their cargoes took away in return hay and straw from the island which were to be sold in London markets.

A ferry across the Colne to Brightlingsea was frequently used by Baring-Gould and his family and the wife of the man who operated it, a certain Mrs. Baker, later found her way into his novel *Mehalah* as Mrs. De Witt. Elijah Rebow, the villain in the same novel, was based on a leading Dissenter at West Mersea. The smuggling activities recorded in *Mehalah* are also based on reality - the intricate network of creeks around the island provided an ideal landscape in which to "move secretly and hide effectively", much as happened at Canvey and Foulness. West Mersea Hall is thought to have been used as a look-out post during the heyday of smuggling activities.

Baring-Gould used to complain that Mersea was always cold and it is fair to say that the sparsely populated eastern end of the island where he lived is rather exposed to winds coming in off the sea. Many outsiders have never visited the island in the winter months, although there are those who would argue that this is when the island is at its best. It is perhaps this atmosphere of cold, desolate isolation which has given rise to a disproportionately high number of ghost stories on Mersea.

The mound at Barrow Hill Farm is the centre of many such legends. It is said, for example, to be guarded by the spirit of a Roman centurion, left behind forever when his legion returned to Rome. Baring-Gould had his own version of the story, writing in *Mehalah* that it contained a ship belonging to a pair of Danish twins who fought to the death over a native British girl and who can still be heard fighting there whenever there is a full moon over the island.

Other spectral sightings on Mersea include the figure of a woman, often seen in the vicinity of the *Dog and Pheasant* inn at East Mersea and thought to have been a victim of murder during the Parliamentarian occupation of Mersea fort, and the 'ghost of the Strood' - a Roman soldier marching along the road to the mainland who is visible only from the waist up, as the road along which he now walks is higher than the level of the old Roman causeway. A cottage at East Mersea, formerly the *Ship* inn, is said to be haunted by the murdered sweetheart of a smuggler - perhaps it is she who some have heard talking when there has been no-one visible there? Ghostly footsteps, laughter, the clatter of horses' hooves and the wheels of Roman chariots have all been witnessed or imagined on Mersea Island.

Shortly after Baring-Gould had left the island a grand scheme was put forward for the construction of extensive docklands, a project which, not surprisingly, when the success of other great Essex island ventures is considered, never actually saw the light of day. The building of Tilbury Docks and Parkeston Quay (see later) elsewhere in the county was responsible for a huge surge in interest in dock construction and many a new scheme was put forward. That for Mersea, introduced in 1887, was for a brand new port called Colnemouth which it was envisaged would be constructed between Ivy House and Mersea Stone at the extreme eastern end of the island. The plan's principal local backer was John Bateman JP of Brightlingsea Hall, one of its biggest selling points being a 730-feet long pier stretching out into Brightlingsea Reach. A 50-feet wide channel, controlled by lock gates, was to lead into a dock about 300 feet wide dug into the end of the island. Successful onward transmission of off-loaded cargo must have been one of the greatest sticking points for the scheme, since the dock, if constructed, would have been at least 11 miles away from the nearest railway, by far the most popular method of overland transport at the time.

A later and much more easily realisable scheme for the construction of a railway line from Mersea to Stanway, near Colchester, in 1919, which would have provided later holidaymakers with a quick and reliable route to the seaside, was similarly ill-fated.

The frontline action which Mersea had seen during the Civil War was surprisingly more than that which it was to see during the otherwise more substantial World War Two as its more northerly position made it less of a target than islands such as Canvey and Foulness for London-bound German bombers who were keen to off-load any surplus cargoes which they still carried over Essex on their return from the Capital. Though bombed several times, the island was most notable for its rôle as a decoy site, known as a 'Q' site (after the famous World War One decoy ships), with which it attracted enemy bombers away from their intended destinations. These sites were built at strategic points around the country to resemble docks, harbours, marshalling yards - anything really which would deceive the enemy into thinking they had hit a genuine target. The role of the Mersea site, which stood near Shop Lane, East Mersea, was to distract aircraft bound for the important minesweeper base at Brightlingsea. The site comprised mock-up buildings made of wood, tubular steel and canvas and carefully positioned lights which simulated a marshalling yard. Oil tanks were also installed and the intention was that these should be set alight by remote control during an air raid to give the impression that the real target had been successfully hit. The site was run by just six men in a camouflaged concrete pillbox.

Although never hit by the enemy, the site was actually destroyed on one occasion by the accidental cutting of electrical wiring when the grass around it was being mown and it had to be rebuilt from scratch.

Apart from the 'Q' site, other concrete coastal defences were also erected at Mersea during the final years of the war as part of a chain of defensive coastal emplacements, but they saw little if any action and were closed down shortly after the war was over. One of them lives on, however, as a popular ice cream parlour on one of today's principal tourist beaches!

The only First World War action the island appears to have seen was in 1916 when a Zeppelin airship crashed at nearby Little Wigborough on the mainland and the crew was marched to Mersea to be locked up before onward transmission to Colchester.

After the Second World War, the Great Tide of 1953 was the next major disaster to hit the island, but because of its comparative height Mersea suffered nowhere near so badly as Canvey or Foulness or the other low-lying coastal areas. The Strood was covered by seven feet of water for several hours and the inundation extended half a mile inland on the nearby mainland as far as the Peldon Rose inn. Mersea was effectively cut off but there was little danger to land and life, although the official who held the keys to the cabinets containing the aptly named 'King Canute' flood rescue operation files did not live on the island and could not gain access to it to set in motion the work that had to be done!

The south-western corner of the island, where most of the boats were moored, was the only seriously affected area. It was an area of houseboats and many of these were broken away from their moorings by the strong supporting winds and blown across the Blackwater estuary to Bradwell. A yacht called the *Ruddy Sheldrake* was actually blown all the way to Holland - 100 miles away! On land, some of the houses in this area were under three feet of floodwater and 20 people were forced to leave their homes until the waters receded.

Whilst the important agricultural land was almost entirely protected from the disaster because it was primarily situated on high ground away from the danger, the oyster industry was devastated as the oysters were covered with silt and mud when the tide eventually went out and were suffocated.

Ten years later the oyster fisheries were hit again when the exceptionally hard winter of 1962-3 froze the creeks in which they were growing and killed literally millions of them. New stock was introduced from elsewhere to prevent the industry from folding altogether but the chronic shortage of oysters which followed led to a long spell of high prices and it was some time before the industry recovered to any significant degree.

Today the oyster fisheries remain an essential part of the island's economy, which is supplemented by income from the considerable yachting and boat-building activities and from tourism, but the 200 fishing smacks which were once the norm here a century ago are no longer present in such numbers. Nevertheless, a popular annual sailing regatta emphasises the island's continued connections with the sea and water-skiing, windsurfing and jet-skiing all take place in the waters around the island.

Popular, too, with sun-seekers, Mersea has one of the lowest rainfall counts in East Anglia, although it also seems to have attracted some of the strangest natural phenomena. In April, 1884, the nearby mainland town of Langenhoe was struck by an earthquake and the effects were felt in some homes on the island. Ninety years later, in 1975, a waterspout, caused by a whirlwind developing over the sea and sucking up water into it, came inland and hurled a small boat some 400 feet through the air.

As with other Essex islands, Mersea is not only popular with humans. The Cudmore Grove Country Park, set up by Essex County Council in 1974 at the eastern end of the island, is home to many species of wild animals and birds. The park contains one of the few substantial bits of woodland on the island and provides a great vantage point for views over the Colne Estuary and its adjacent nature reserve on the opposite bank of the river. An information room gives details of what to see in the park and bridleways and picnic sites are also provided for complementary recreational activities. Several World War II pill-boxes survive within the park, whilst the broken remains of associated gun emplacements can be found on the beach below after coastal erosion of the cliffs which once supported them. The cliffs have revealed fossils dating back 300,000 years. An average of 150,000 people visit the park every year.

Thousands of youngsters also come from all over the world to stay at the nearby Essex County Council-run East Mersea International Youth Camp, which was set up in the 1930s by a rich London builder as a place of education and holidaying for East End children. The site was taken over by the army in the war and the Youth Camp replaced the original operation once it was over. Members of the Hitler Youth were amongst the many post-war visitors, being 'treated' there for de-Nazification. The camp is no longer restricted to underprivileged East End children and offers a wide variety of educational and recreational opportunities, including sports, boating, camping and obstacle courses.

Like Canvey, Mersea has its own museum, next to the church in West Mersea, which houses a collection of island bygones and marine-related items. It does not, however, have such facilities as a hospital or a cinema and residents have to travel to Colchester for those. A golf course once existed at East Mersea, but this has long since been closed down and the clubhouse is now a private residence.

The height of the island is underlined by the fact that there was once a windmill there, built at an advantageous elevation to catch the wind as it blew in off the north sea, and also by the presence of an old brick water tower, built in 1924 to overcome the problems of making clean drinking water available to the growing population. The water on Mersea was always known by outsiders to be 'funny', possessing a strange taste which visitors could never get used to.

Many observers believe that although Mersea is likely to be busiest in the summer months, a visit out of season in autumn or winter (complete with essential suitable attire for keeping out the cold) is the most rewarding, for this is when the island is at its best. Certainly Mersea somehow seems to have a little more to offer every time you visit it and it is undoubtedly well worth a visit for those who have never been there. It offers a comforting mix of commercialism and solitude, a reassuring feeling of safety and yet an apprehension at the unknown.

James Wentworth Day summed it up well with his romantic description of Mersea as "...the Isle the Romans knew, the Danes held, the Germans bombed six hundred times and England has never yet quite conquered..."

The Mersea 'City' area at West Mersea

## MERSEA'S SMALLER ISLANDS

*"A more desolate region can scarce be conceived, and yet it is not without beauty."*

SABINE BARING-GOULD, *Mehalah*

There are at least ten other islands in the vicinity of Mersea Island, all small and marshy but some very historic and each worthy of interest in its own right.

### GREAT COB ISLAND AND LITTLE COB ISLAND

To the south-west of Mersea Island lies a maze of creeks and channels which provide sea access for the two mainland maritime villages of Tollesbury and Salcott-cum-Virley. The former is accessed by Tollesbury Fleet, the latter by Salcott Channel.

Tollesbury Fleet is home to two adjacent long narrow islands, running parallel to each other, north-west to south-east in the middle of the river. These are Great Cob Island and Little Cob Island, the two largest of a handful of raised marshland areas in the Fleet which separate the river's North and South Channels. This is a popular leisure waterway and the area in the vicinity of the two islands is used as an anchorage for boats. In former times, the islands were also popular with wildfowlers and were known during this activity as 'holes'.

### SAMPHIRE (OR 'SUNKEN') ISLAND

Salcott Channel is home to only one major island, but its history and interest is far more significant than that of the islands in Tollesbury Fleet. Samphire or 'Sunken' Island is said to have been the location for the murder one night of a 'boat load' of excisemen during the rough smuggling heyday of Mersea Island, a trade which thrived in the maze of creeks and islands hereabouts. The excisemen, whose ghosts are still said to haunt the island, discovered a smuggling run in mid-progress and were promptly dealt with by the lawless smugglers.

More recently, at the end of 1997, the island was sold to a private buyer for a reported £65,000. The purchase included the title of Lord (or Lady) of the Manor of Great Wigborough-cum-Salcott (two mainland villages), plus mineral rights and rent from a wildfowl shooting club.  A visit to the island at high tide amply demonstrates how it got its 'sunken' nickname, as very little of it is actually visible above the surface!

The name, 'Samphire' Island, comes from an abundant, edible plant which grows there (and on other islands in the vicinity), also known as 'sea asparagus'.  The island is part of a Site of Special Scientific Interest (SSSI) and, despite its regular flooding, has significant wildlife value for seabirds.

PACKING SHEDS ISLAND

Just to the east of Samphire Island is Packing Sheds Island (sometimes recorded in historic documents as Packing House or Packing Marsh Island), which gets its name from the fact that it is home to a shed where oysters were formerly packed and stored.  The island is still owned by the Mersea & Tollesbury Oyster Fishery Company but is leased to the Packing Shed Trust, which was set up in 1991 to restore the packing shed and use both it and the island for local community benefit.

The shed at the time was in a bad state of disrepair and was falling over into the water.  Local residents and representatives from the International Youth Camp on Mersea Island got together to raise funds and set about restoring it.  Despite its apparent bad condition, the underlying construction of the shed, with a supporting wooden base and sturdy mortise and tenon joints, showed that it had actually been very soundly made. (It is thought to date from the 1870s.) A second shed once existed, but this was supported by concrete pillars and, when a high tide came in 1915, it simply lifted the shed off its supports and floated it away!  Today's shed creates a similar 'floating' illusion when seen from Mersea Island at high tide, but its exposed position in the estuary belies the evident strength of its support.

Photographs inside the shed, which now houses a museum of artifacts related to the history of the island - mainly connected with the oyster industry, whose pits still scar the landscape there - clearly show the amount of work that was put in to restore the building and bring it back into use after just one year. Since then it has hosted numerous functions, including barbecues, yacht racing meetings, a 90th birthday party and even a wedding!  Three thousand visitors a year now pass through the shed courtesy of the Packing Shed Trust, which also hosts cream teas there during the annual Mersea Regatta.

The island itself is not a big one, but it and the shed were once home to 30 men working in the oyster industry.  The oysters were grown in pits on the

Cindery Island (left) with Thames barge

Inside the old packing shed, now a museum-cum-entertainment area, Packing Sheds Island

island and loaded into a stationary barge next to the shed, where they could be stored for onward transmission to other barges. The stationary barge is still there, but it has rotted away over the years and is now just a wooden hull, visible at low tide. Little terns nest on the island, which, though low-lying, is rarely flooded completely - perhaps twice in 10 years.

Packing Sheds Island is no longer actively used in the oyster industry, but oysters are still cultivated by the Mersea & Tollesbury Oyster Fishery Company in the waters around the western end of Mersea Island - sticks marking their positions can be seen protruding from the water at high tide. A surprising 14 species of plant do, however, inhabit the little island, six of which are sufficiently rare to be notifiable and protected.

The island is suffering from coastal erosion and the Environment Agency is overseeing a scheme to recharge it with stone brought in from Harwich harbour.

## COBMARSH ISLAND

Immediately to the east of Packing Sheds Island is Cobmarsh island, another island formerly used in oyster cultivation. This is a larger island, closer to (and thus easily visible from) West Mersea, but still generally low-lying and marshy.

It is said that Cobmarsh and Packing Sheds Islands were once connected by a strip of land across the water and that it was possible to walk a horse and cart across between them. There is, however, no evidence of such a 'road' there now.

Like Packing Sheds Island, Cobmarsh is valuable for wildlife and floods completely only rarely. There are notices on the island warning the many yachtsmen who inhabit these parts against landing there during the summer breeding season so as not to disturb the birds.

There is little else of interest on Cobmarsh Island, but it might have some future value as an area for boat moorings if erosion takes place more dramatically than at present.

## RAY ISLAND

To the north-west of Mersea, in the Strood Channel which separates that island from the mainland, is Ray Island. At 100 acres this is the largest and arguably the most important in terms of wildlife of the smaller islands in this vicinity. A long, narrow tapering area of marshland, stretching westwards from the Strood and only cut off from the mainland at times of high tide, it is a significant wildlife area, designated as an SSSI and a nature reserve and owned by the National Trust and managed by the Essex Wildlife Trust.

It consists of saltings merging into rough grassland, with a shingly foreshore and higher land containing blackthorn thickets and hawthorn.  There is a wide range of saltmarsh plants, including golden samphire and sea rush.  The thickets provide good cover for nesting, migrant and roosting birds and wildfowl and waders are numerous in winter, when short-eared owls are also frequently seen.  It is even home to pasture land for sheep!

The whole island is well-known as a good example of natural land development where, because it lies in a sheltered estuary, it has not been eroded to  form a cliff but a gentle slope of first marshland, then grassland, then woodland beyond.  Dr. P. H. Reaney gives the name as meaning "at the low-lying land", though this is actually probably the highest of all the smaller west-end Mersea islands!

This is the island where Mehalah, the heroine of East Mersea rector, Sabine Baring-Gould's novel of that name, had her home - "a small farmhouse built of tarred wreckage timber and roofed with red pan tiles".  Are the apple trees that grow there relics of Mehalah's garden ...?

Mehalah was not the first occupant of Ray Island - two 'Red Hills' provide evidence of Roman occupation and the ghostly Roman centurion who allegedly haunts the Strood is also said to have been seen on the island.

Access by foot to Ray Island is by a path across the adjacent and privately-owned Bonner's Saltings, which starts at the northern end of the Strood almost opposite Strood Villa.  Any planned visit to either should be arranged through the island's warden and care should be taken with planning for tides.

## PEWIT ISLAND

To the north-east of Mersea Island, in the Pyefleet Channel on the other side of the Strood, is Pewit Island.  The second of the three 'peewit' islands in this geographical tour around the county, it also takes its name from the peewit bird.

Shown in some 17th century documents as 'Puit' Island, it has also been recorded in later reports as 'Peewit' Island (two 'e's).

Despite its small size, Pewit Island once had an important rôle to play in the calendar of civic events of the nearby mainland town of Colchester, as it was home to the oyster packing shed which for many years was used by the Mayor of Colchester to conduct the town's ancient annual oyster ceremony. The shed, an old Nissen hut (replacing an earlier building burnt down in the 1940s), is still there, but it has recently become too dilapidated for use and the ceremony now takes place on a barge in the vicinity of the island instead of on it.

This ceremony, in October, features local civic dignitaries, invited guests and, on occasion, members of the Royal Family. It is followed by an Oyster Feast in Colchester itself and dates back in its present form to the early Victorian period.

Signs of the old oyster industry can still be seen on the island as its surface is marked by old oyster pits. It is owned by Colchester Borough Council but leased to the Colchester Oyster Fishery, which operates from a base across the creek on Mersea Island.

## LANGENHOE ISLAND

To the immediate north of Pewit Island - between the Pyefleet Channel (north of Mersea) and Geedon Creek (a tributary of the River Colne) - is a long promontory which is noted in some documents as 'Langenhoe Island'.

Following the construction of a seawall and the reclamation of land, however, this is no longer really an island at all and cannot in any case be visited as it is part of a Ministry of Defence firing range. Seen from above or on a map, it seems to mirror Ray Island to the west (itself now absorbed into the mainland as a long promontory at all but high tide), though it is of less historic and natural significance.

Dotted with creeks, the area that is now behind the seawall was once several low-lying, flat marshy areas, but these have all been absorbed into one.

## RAT ISLAND

To the immediate north of Langenhoe 'Island', in the mouth of Geedon Creek, is Rat Island. This is a raised area of marshland covering some 35 acres, primarily saltings, and is an important nature reserve. It is the site of the county's largest nesting colony of black-headed gulls (over 4,000 pairs were counted there in the mid-1980s) and is also home to a small colony of common terns. The area is designated as a Site of Special Scientific Interest (SSSI) and no visiting is allowed. The gull colony has been threatened, however, by increased tidal inundation and there has been some migration to areas on the adjacent mainland marshland.

The island is owned by Colchester Borough Council, but leased to the Essex Wildlife Trust whose headquarters is sited nearby on the mainland at Fingringhoe Wick. Apart from approaches by water, the best view of the island is to be had from across the Colne on the footpath walk from Brightlingsea which follows the course of the old Wivenhoe-Brightlingsea railway. The mainland on the Rat Island side of the Colne is Ministry of Defence property and cannot be accessed.

CINDERY ISLAND

To the east of Mersea Island, across the River Colne in Brightlingsea Creek within sight of Brightlingsea town, lies Cindery Island. The original low-lying marshland island has been broken into two by the force of the tide flowing from St Osyth Creek to the south. It is said locally that this action was exacerbated by a former owner of St Osyth Priory cutting a part of the island away to allow his yacht to manoeuvre into the creek. Some attempts are being made to join the two halves of the island together again by filling the gap with hardcore. The former single island can be clearly seen on Chapman & André's map of Essex of 1777.

According to Dr. P. H. Reaney, the island's name derives from the Old English *sundor eg*, meaning "apart low-lying land". As with other islands in the locality, it is laced with a number of oyster pits, now largely disused. The main channel to the south of the island is usually lined with boats - a symbol of Brightlingsea's maritime history and a reminder of the town's rôle as a wartime minesweeper base when military vessels anchored in the waters there.

It is worth mentioning here that the town of Brightlingsea itself was once an island, being marked as such on county maps until as recently as the 16th century.

Even as late as the 18th century the Essex historian, Philip Morant, recorded that it was "very nearly an island". Today, the course of Alresford Creek, inland behind the town, has been altered and it would surely now be only at times of very severe flood that Brightlingsea would ever be cut off from the rest of the mainland.

Cindery Island from Brightlingsea

## THE WALTON BACKWATERS & THE RIVER STOUR

The last group of islands on this geographical tour of the county is in the north-east corner near Harwich.

All but one of them are part of a close-knit group situated in an area known as the Walton Backwaters - a maze of creeks and channels between Harwich and Walton.  There are many 'island-like' areas of marshland in this vicinity, but only about 10 of them really qualify as islands.  Numerous others that look like they might be islands are actually parts of larger (and real) islands and are revealed as such at low tide.  The whole of the Backwaters area has remained largely un-touched by human intervention and Nature is consequently very much in charge there.

The one remaining island that is not in the Backwaters grouping is Ray Island in the River Stour.  Though no longer a proper island (it is now part of the mainland) it is nevertheless perhaps the most important island in the north-east part of the county for Mankind, since it is home to Parkeston Quay and the Harwich International Port from where ferry services depart for Holland and Scandinavia.

With its mix of natural wonder and human industry, this Walton Backwaters and the River Stour group of islands is a very diverse and interesting one on which to end the tour.

Chapman & André map, 1777

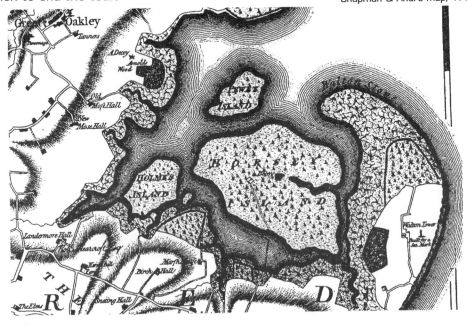

## THE WALTON BACKWATERS

*"I don't suppose the people in the town ever dream they're so near the Secret Water."*

ARTHUR RANSOME, *Secret Water*

The Walton Backwaters is the name given to the maze of constantly changing creeks and low-lying marshland islands immediately to the north west of the popular seaside resort of Walton-on-the-Naze. It was immortalised in the 1939 novel *Secret Water* by *Swallows and Amazons* author, Arthur Ransome, who obviously knew the area well and refers to many of the islands in his story.

Largely undeveloped, the Backwaters is an area of significant environmental importance, especially for wading birds and wildfowl. It has consequently been designated as the Hamford Water Site of Special Scientific Interest (SSSI) - Hamford Water is the main creek which runs through the area. Skipper's Island, in particular, is an important area for formal wildlife conservation. The dynamic nature of the terrain throughout the Backwaters means that it can be very dangerous to negotiate for people who are not familiar with the area.

The principal islands in the area are grouped around Hamford Water which, at its furthest extent, reaches some four miles inland. Hamford is actually just one of a multitude of creeks in the Backwaters, which has often been described as a "riverless estuary", since it is fed only by three small brooks which emerge as Great Oakley Creek in the north, Kirby Creek in the south and Walton Channel in the south-east. The south-west corner also features a small channel, leading to the now-disued Beaumont Quay, whilst in between the islands there are numerous other smaller waterways.

The whole area was known as long ago as Roman times, the Romans using Beaumont Quay as a port and building a road from there initially to Colchester and on to their wider road network which spanned the south eastern corner of the country. As at many other Essex coastal sites, including Canvey, Foulness, Osea and certain other of the county's islands, they also introduced salt-making facilities and the 'Red Hills' which are thought to be the last visible remains of this salt-making process can be seen on Horsey and Skipper's Islands in the Backwaters.

Later, in Saxon times, Hamford Water was known as 'Fullanpettae', suggested derivations of which include both "fowl pit" and "foul pit". From contemporary observations it seems that both derivations were justified! There even appears to have been some occupation of the area during the Bronze Age as a number of arrowheads dating from that period have been found in the Backwaters.

More recently, the quays at Landermere and Great Oakley were famous as destinations for sailing barges, the latter in particular becoming a departure point for regular sailings to London before the advent of the railways.

Getting a good land-based view of the Backwaters' 2,000 or so acres is not easy. Some of the best views can be had from the B1034 between Kirby and Walton, or from the crumbling clifftops of the Naze, 80 feet above sea level and topped by a tower of similar height which is used as a navigational landmark. Even views from a boat can be inconclusive, since the creeks, the islands and the mainland all seem to blend into one.

Just exactly how many raised areas of land in this constantly changing marshland area constitute genuine islands is difficult to determine, since the whole area is very low-lying and patches of marshland which are above the water at some tides can easily be below it at others. It is generally accepted that there are 10 areas which qualify as islands in the Backwaters.

## HORSEY ISLAND

The largest and most obvious island in the Backwaters is Horsey Island, so named, according to Dr. P. H. Reaney, because it was used for some time as an enclosure for horses. There has, however, also been some suggestion that the name might be derived from Danish occupation (by confusion of the term 'Norse' with 'horse') and that it was used in a similar way to Mersea and Northey Islands as a base for the launching of invading Viking forces on to the Essex mainland.

Though set at some considerable distance out into the middle of the Backwaters (immediately to the south of the main inlet of Hamford Water and to the west of the second largest creek, the Walton Channel), the island is nevertheless comparatively easily accessible at low tide as a long causeway connects it to the mainland. This causeway, known as Island Road and in existence since at least 1777, is even able to support vehicular traffic. Be warned, however, that the causeway is both very dangerous and private, so no-one should attempt the crossing without prior planning and permission.

In the 18th and 19th centuries Horsey saw use as pasture land for sheep, which had occasionally to be 'swum' from the mainland if the state of the tide was unfavourable for the causeway. In the 20th century some arable farming took place, though sheep and horses are currently bred there as before.

The causeway to Horsey Island

Hedge End Island from the mainland marina

Causeway to the mainland from Skipper's Island

Horsey is the most prominently featured of the Backwaters' islands in Arthur Ransome's *Secret Water*, in which it is referred to as 'Swallow Island'. The dangerous tidal waterway between the island and the mainland is 'The Red Sea', whilst the landing area at Kirby-le-Soken to the south is 'Witch's Quay'. The sheltered creek which provides a good anchorage point between Horsey and neighbouring Skipper's Island is given the name of 'Goblin Creek'.

Ransome is not the only author to have been inspired by the Backwaters. Hamford Water, for example, is featured in the 1888 novel *Richard Cable* which was written by the East Mersea rector, Sabine Baring-Gould.

Apart from its farming uses (there is still a farmhouse on the island), Horsey's importance today is largely in respect of its wonderful natural heritage. Many rare species of seabird winter in this area, particularly Brent Geese. Curlews, herons, oystercatchers and redshank are amongst the many other bird species seen there. There was once a large colony of gulls on the island, but the constant unchecked attentions of foxes have led to a significant decline in the gull population there in recent years.

Being low-lying, Horsey Island was flooded by the Great Tide in 1953, but the walls did not give in (they were overtopped). It was also one of the few areas affected by flooding four years later, under Hurricane 'Carrie'.

Horsey is a large island and this, and the two or three buildings that are on it, help the eye to pick it out fairly easily from the surrounding islands and marshland.

## HEDGE END ISLAND

To the east of Horsey Island, on the edge of the Walton Channel, is Hedge End Island, which is separated from the mainland to the south by a stretch of water known as The Twizzle. This is a popular boating area giving access to the Backwaters' principal yacht harbour (Titchmarsh Marina) and is a frequent anchoring point for the Walton Lifeboat. The area around the island is often filled with yachts and yachtsmen, particularly during the summer months.

The most easterly of the genuine islands in the centre of the Backwaters, Hedge End is also the closest to the built-up area of Walton town and the popular recreational area of the adjacent Naze. Despite this, however, little of the island's history seems to have been recorded and it is today simply a medium-sized marshland island with some embanked seawalls.

It seems likely that Hedge End was once part of Horsey Island but became separated from it during the Black Monday floods of November, 1897, which affected other islands in the Backwaters, transforming them from grazing land for sheep to simple marshland.

## STANDCREEK SALTS

Standcreek Salts is an area of saltmarsh immediately to the north of Hedge End Island which to all intents and purposes looks identical to Hedge End and the two in truth were probably once one. It is separated from Hedge End by Salt Creek and from Horsey to the west by the curiously named channel of 'The Dardanelles'.

## SKIPPER'S ISLAND

To the west of Horsey Island is Skipper's Island, one of the most significant in the Backwaters. Skipper's lies closer geographically to the mainland at Kirby-le-Soken than Horsey and is divided from the latter by the trailing course of Kirby Creek. This creek is one of the most sheltered areas in the Backwaters and, before its development as a haunt for pleasure-boats, it was once used by queues of barges, up to five at a time, which would temporarily anchor there while waiting for a berth to become free at one of the nearby mainland quays.

In the 19th century and earlier the island was known as Holmes Island, but no truly convincing explanation has yet been given as to the reason for the change. (The word 'holm' translates as "river island".) Peter Ford, in his book *Tendring Peninsula*, observes that whilst the island was originally shown as Holmes Island in the maps of John Oliver (1696), Chapman and André (1777) and Greenwood (1824), it was marked as "Skipper's or Holmes Island" on an army map of 1805, when the area was being surveyed in preparation for an anticipated invasion by Napoleon. The placing of "Skipper's" first, suggests Mr. Ford, implies that this name was in most common use at the time, whilst the retention of the name "Holmes" continued to indicate the island's earlier designation. By the time of the publication of the 1875 Ordnance Survey map, however, it was shown solely as Skipper's Island.

Amongst the theories put forward to explain the change of name is the romantic notion that, in the olden days when the Backwaters was a busy commercial shipping destination, barges using Landermere Quay would stop at the island to allow their captain or 'skipper' to jump off the ship with any smuggled contraband which he had in his possession and there let him wait out of sight until the vessel had been cleared by Customs, after which it would be safe for him to climb back on board.

More likely is the theory that the island was named after the Skipper family who lived in Kirby-le-Soken in the second half of the 18th century, owning much of the land in the area. Holmes Island, as it was then, was certainly taken over for rental by a certain John Skipper in 1758 (Arthur Ransome calls is Mastodon Island in *Secret Water* - a name based purely on the storyline of the novel).

Like much of the larger Horsey Island to the east (and other Essex islands such as Mersea), the highest parts of Skipper's Island consist primarily of London clay, which is covered by rough pasture, bushes and scrub. There is also a handful of small freshwater pools on the island. A once-thriving heronry has now disappeared but the small wooded area in which the herons lived still remains, although the predominance of elm trees, most of which were affected by the dreaded Dutch Elm disease in the 1970s, has seen it sadly depleted. The island's lower areas, once farmed with wheat and also used for grazing, began to revert to saltmarsh before the commencement of the Second World War due to the failure to repair a series of breaches in the seawall which had been caused by a succession of high flood tides (including the Black Monday floods of 1897). An attempt to use Skipper's for grazing again during the war years proved unsuccessful as the cattle which were being kept there had a tendency to stray off the island into the surrounding mud. The floods of 1953 ultimately put paid to any ideas for the re-establishment of grazing there on a long-term basis as almost all of the Backwaters, Skipper's Island included, was flooded for several days. Breaches made then have never been repaired.

Now a reserve of the Essex Wildlife Trust, Skipper's Island covers some 233 acres (including surrounding saltmarsh) and it is well-known by ornithologists as the haunt of black-headed gulls, Brent Geese, curlew, gadwall, godwit, kestrels, nightingales, short-eared owls, oystercatchers, redshank, shelduck and many other interesting species. Three areas of dense woodland thickets also provide cover for rabbits, pheasants and foxes.

It is also home to a thriving insect and plant population. Fisher's estuarine (or frosted orange) moth, which was discovered in the Backwaters only as recently as 1968 by J. B. Fisher, is resident there and indeed it is the only large moth whose sole British population is to be found in Essex. Its caterpillar feeds on the stem of a plant called sea hog's fennel and this plant is itself extremely rare, growing at only one other known location in the country, a site near Faversham in Kent. The relatively recent discovery and consequent rarity value of the moth has meant that its pupae are rather coveted by moth collectors and there have been cases on the island where illegal digging for these pupae has been found to be taking place. The feathered ranunculus and rosy wave moths, the Essex Skipper butterfly (perhaps a feature in the island's renaming?) and Roesel's bush cricket are other important insects which live on the Skipper's reserve. As for mammals, frequent sightings of the common seal are made in the area.

It is largely because of the wealth of wildlife on Skipper's Island that the Backwaters has been designated a Site of Special Scientific Interest (SSSI) and a National Nature Reserve (NNR).

Since first leasing Skipper's Island in 1972 from the then owner and well-known naturalist, Fred Williams, the Essex Wildlife Trust has put a lot of work into managing the reserve, introducing footpaths and clearings and carrying out much-needed repairs to the seawalls. The pools and grassland of the island have been given particular attention as they provide homes for a wide range of animal and plant life.

Mr. Williams, an authority on butterflies and moths, first acquired Skipper's Island in the mid-1950s and spent much of his time actually living there. He even encouraged members of the Essex Field Club to carry out their own wildlife surveys and some of their findings were published in the *Essex Naturalist* conservation magazine.

Access to Skipper's Island is not permitted without prior arrangement - the access route from the main road is in any case in private ownership - and even then, when prior arrangement has been made, it is not the easiest of islands to get to. A short causeway across to the island is "negotiable at low tide by a reasonably agile person in wellingtons", but a boat is really the best means of making the crossing. An array of 'Private' notices is designed to deter the unwelcome visitor.

In recent years, the Trust has rented out Mr. Williams' cottage (still known as 'Fred's') and Trust members are able to stay on the island. This provides a fascinating experience of a wildlife paradise where Mankind is thankfully restricted to being a privileged, temporary and very fortunate visitor.

HONEY ISLAND

In the middle of Kirby Creek between the much larger Horsey and Skipper's Islands is Honey Island, one of the smallest, if not the very smallest, of all the genuine islands in the Backwaters. It is also one of the best examples of an island here, despite its small size, because it is constantly surrounded by water at all states of the tide, whereas many of the other larger islands can be approached across the mud when the tide is out. Even so, Honey Island is too small to do much with and does not constitute much more than an oval patch of low-lying marshland, popular with seabirds.

The derivation of the 'Honey' designation is unclear. Arthur Ransome calls it 'Bridget Island' in *Secret Water*, named after one of the characters.

## PEWIT ISLAND

On the other side of Hamford Water is Pewit Island, the third island of that name in the county in this geographical tour. The most northerly of the Backwaters' islands, it lies just to the east of Oakley Creek and almost certainly owes its name to the call of the peewit bird, a type of plover which thrives on the habitat such as is present in this area. There is an old story that the annual arrival of these birds on the island always took place on St George's Day - quite why is unclear!

One of only three islands in the Backwaters to be shown on Chapman and André's 1777 map (Horsey and Skipper's Islands being the other two), it was shown then as "Pewet Island". In 1804, however, it was shown on some maps as "Powet Island" and it has also been referred to in other sources as "Peewit Island" (two 'e's).

On a map produced for Samuel Pepys in 1686 (later passed to the Walton Heritage Centre) it is described as "Fowley Island", though where this name came from (apart from the likely alternative bird derivation) is unclear.

Unlike many of the other large islands in the Backwaters, Pewit has no sea defences and is therefore now little more than an area of unprotected, low-lying marshland. It seems to have been lost to the sea in 1897 - a writer from the Essex Naturalist who visited the area in 1898 reported that following that year's flooding Pewit Island was now "derelict and unusable". Forty years later this and other islands in the Backwaters were again underwater following prolonged off-shore storms. Sheet steel piling at other islands, particularly Bramble Island (see below), has gone some way to preventing further inundations, but a repetition of anything like the Great Tide of 1953 would almost certainly swamp Pewit.

## NEW ISLAND

Immediately to the south of Pewit Island lies New Island, very similar in make-up and appearance to its northern neighbour. The name 'New' suggests that it is of comparatively recent appearance and indeed the island would seem to have come into existence in 1897 when the Black Monday floods of November that year swamped Pewit Island and broke it into two.

Pewit and New Islands are collectively shown as 'Peewitland' in Arthur Ransome's *Secret Water*, an indication that even then there were those who remembered the two islands being one.

## GARNHAM'S ISLAND

To the south and west of New Island is Garnham's Island, actually little more than a disorganised cluster of small, low-lying marshland areas, many of which are under water during high tide.

The Garnham derivation is thought to come from a former owner, perhaps in the 19th century when it was used as pasture land for sheep. The island was completely destroyed, however, by the Black Monday floods of November 1897 and any hope of reclaiming it was killed off by further flooding in 1928 at which stage it was simply abandoned to the sea. Arthur Ransome calls it 'Blackberry Island' in *Secret Water*, but it is now little more than marshland.

It is thought to be Garnham's Island that the 18th century Essex historian, Philip Morant, was referring to when he mentioned an area in the Backwaters called 'Sunk Island', so it must have suffered extensive flooding on a previous occasion prior to 1897.

## BRAMBLE ISLAND

To the west of Pewit Island lies Bramble Island, which is technically no longer an island at all. Old maps show it predominantly as marshland, separate from the mainland, and at one stage (until c.1875) it and Garnham's Island were one. But Bramble was reclaimed in the late 19th century and a seawall was built around it, enclosing it into the mainland.

Up to the late 19th century the main use for Bramble Island appears to have been as pasture land for sheep, but in 1897 the island was flooded (like others in the Backwaters) and the sheep on it were drowned. The surveyor who visited Pewit Island in 1898 also visited Bramble and reported that the seawall had been breached and had still not been repaired, converting irretrievably former pasture land into "an enormous waste of black rotting mud and weeds".

Shortly after this disaster, however, probably later in 1898, the High Explosives Company (HEC) bought the island and began the manufacture of explosives there. The location was chosen partly because of its remoteness from population, partly because of the cheapness of the land and partly because of the ease of access by water for the transportation of materials. It would appear that it was HEC which began the formal reclamation of the land and the construction of the seawalls.

By 1905, however, HEC had been declared bankrupt and the island was bought by Explosives & Chemical Products Ltd. (ECP), part of a French-owned company which took over HEC's licence. In those early days some of the brick buildings on the island were actually built from bricks made in situ with its clay.

The main access route to the island at this time was from the west via Old Moze Hall, owned c.1906 by Guy's Hospital and tenanted by Mr. Joy, whose name lives on in 'Joy's Dock' nearby. The main entrance today was little more than a lane leading down from Great Oakley to another dock in the Backwaters to the north of the island ('Great Oakley Dock' and the main one now in use), but this stopped well short of the island itself. Both docks had seen much use throughout the 19th century in the heyday of barge traffic in Hamford Water, with barges bringing in manure from London streets to spread on the land and 'exporting' the resulting hay that had grown there from the mainland farms.

Materials transported over land were taken via Old Moze Hall to Thorpe-le-Soken railway station or carried on a small gauge railway to the main Great Oakley Dock where they were transferred onto lorries and taken up Dock Lane to Harwich port. There was also some loading later at Mistley railway station.

There was some early friction between the industrialists and the local farmers, as local people who had traditionally been employed in agriculture began instead to look for employment at the factory as the dangerous nature of the work there commanded a better wage. The early years of activity at Bramble were fairly small-scale, though the peace of the neighbourhood was shattered in May 1913 by an explosion at the factory which claimed the life of one of its employees. Barely three weeks later the British Explosives Syndicate at Pitsea Hall Island also suffered an explosion and ECP sent their compatriots a message of condolence.

The First World War led to an expansion of the factory, when a shortage of explosives on the Western Front increased the urgency for their production.

In 1915 the Admiralty constructed a new road from the bottom of Dock Lane onto the island and provided a new jetty on the eastern side (close to an existing one) jutting out into the Backwaters. Men with explosives knowledge were sent back from the front and the island was guarded by 30 soldiers. The new road, originally a cinder track, was not concreted until the late 1920s. Amongst the most significant developments at this stage was the production here of some of the first anti-submarine depth-charge material. At about this time the island was also given its own borehole (for water) and boilers were rolled across the fields for installation from Joy's Dock.

Halfway through the Great War ECP began to experiment with explosives for coal mining and by the end of the war the company had established itself as one of the foremost producers of explosives for the mining and quarrying industries.

Everything was going well until 1928 when floods along the east coast breached the seawall during the night and caused substantial damage to the factory. The seawall was repaired and Bramble Island saved, but Garnham's Island, already ruined by the 1897 inundation, was given up for good. A second explosion, in 1929, added to the misery of this late-1920s period.

With the Second World War approaching, ECP bought Great Oakley Hall, consolidating with it the purchase of Old Moze Hall and thus providing a substantial agricultural buffer zone between the factory and the mainland community. New buildings were erected and schemes for their camouflage tried out in anticipation of German bombing. By 1940 the factory was at its busiest, with 230-240 people being employed there. Much expansion had taken place since the 1920s, with new roads and buildings and new explosives and technologies. An employees' bus service was laid on in 1941, replacing the hordes of cyclists who used to come in, and the severe winter of 1940 even provided the novel experience of being able to walk across the frozen sea to Garnham's Island. A third explosion in 1942 was the only real dampener on activities.

After the war the factory was able to make use of newly-discovered German technology. It was also connected to the mains electricity system (the grid) and Great Oakley Dock was dug out to provide greater depth for shipping.

The 1950s, however, brought several disasters. A fourth explosion in 1950 claimed three lives, as did a fifth (thankfully the last to have occurred there) in 1956.

In between these two incidents came a totally unexpected disaster - the Great Tide of 1953. Bramble Island had been described by the engineer to the Essex Rivers Catchment Board shortly before the Great Tide as "particularly vulnerable" to flooding and this observation was unfortunately to come true with disastrous consequences. As the floodwaters rose, the seawalls were breached, with the water spilling into the factory and carrying explosives around as it went. A nightwatchman guarding the factory drowned in the flood and his body was not found for several days when it was washed ashore 10 miles up the coast. Attempts both to locate him and investigate the damage to the factory were seriously hampered by the large number of partly-submerged and floating explosives.

Water covered most of the island for several days after the flood, to a depth of three feet even at low tide. Despite this, however, the main breaches in the seawalls were successfully sealed within seven days, though the walls themselves still needed further strengthening.

During the flooding over 40 wooden buildings were destroyed or moved. One was even carried over the counterwall at the back of the island and out onto the mainland half a mile beyond. Another came to a rest on top of the seawall. Some explosive components and storage barrels floated across Hamford Water to Horsey Island a mile away and, quite remarkably, some even washed up on the shore at Margate, a considerable distance further than that!

One of the main problems with the rescue operation at Bramble was that the site was entirely self-contained so that all electric, gas and water services were out of action. Even so, the factory remained inoperative for only six weeks, though it took some 18 months before the entire site was fully cleared.

In all, up to 150 tons of explosive material was wasted, most of it later being dumped in the sea at a specially designated site some eight miles off the coast. A specially adapted Second World War Mulberry Harbour barge was fitted out for the purpose, but even this had to stand for several days alongside the factory waiting for calm enough seas to travel to the dumping ground to ensure that no explosion took place *en route*. A location originally planned for the dumping - 13 miles out from the Suffolk coastal town of Orford - was rejected because of the danger inherent in taking the load such a distance. The journey to the final resting place, in the vicinity of the Cork Light Vessel, itself involved a difficult passage through the narrow creeks of the Backwaters and the scuttling of the explosive-laden barge, once the dumping ground had eventually been reached, took an agonizing 71 minutes to complete. The area is now marked by a special buoy, the explosives themselves lying over 40 feet down below it. Three factory employees involved in the clear-up operations in 1953 were each awarded the British Empire Medal. Factory diaries record that Hilda Grieve, author of *The Great Tide*, the definitive account of the tragedy, visited the island on 11th March, 1958.

As time went on the demand for commercial explosives began to decrease and ECP began to look at alternative ventures. Perhaps the most surprising was the development in the 1970s of a food production plant, complete with hens, pigs and potato chips, the latter grown on the company's local farmland.

The manufacture of explosives at Bramble Island ceased in 1985 and ECP's successor, Exchem Organics, today produces intermediate chemical products for a wide range of industries, all largely based on the successful nitration process developed during explosives manufacture. Speciality chemicals, such as environmentally-friendly diesel fuel additives, plus components for hair dyes, antibiotics, photographic and X-ray film processing and printing cartridges are all manufactured on the site. In 1997 a metal-recovery plant was introduced and in 1998 an open day attracted 1,400 people!

The current factory site occupies 180 acres (though Exchem owns a total of 1,000 acres with the surrounding farmland). It employs around 80 people.

Despite the industrial activity, Bramble Island is home to a surprising number of wildlife species, including the rare Fisher's estuarine moth and the hog's fennel plant on which it feeds. The moth is unique to the Backwaters, whilst the plant is known only here and at one site in Faversham (Kent). It is thought that it was probably brought here from Faversham in brick rubble by barge. Brent Geese, seabirds, owls and seals are amongst the many other creatures seen in the locality. Exchem takes its wildlife responsibilities seriously and is a corporate member of the Essex Wildlife Trust.

The development of explosives in the Backwaters has not been limited to Bramble Island, as research work on the development of experimental rockets was once also carried out on the marshes below the navigational tower on the mainland at Walton-on-the-Naze. Exploding rockets would often light up the entire area while being test-fired on a miniature railway.

## STONE MARSH/STONE POINT

Beyond all these islands, off the very tip of the Naze, curving like a barrier to keep them all in place, is a little row of unnamed marshland islands which culminates in the promontory known as Stone Marsh or Stone Point on the edge of Pennyhole Bay.

The very tip of Stone Point features a one-and-a-half mile long curving shingle spit, which is an important nesting site for little terns and other shore birds. The site is regularly policed by wardens throughout the breeding season, a practice carried out jointly by the Essex Wildlife Trust (EWT) and the Essex Birdwatching and Preservation Society (EBPS), and forms part of the Trust's nine-acre John Weston Reserve.

This is also a very popular leisure spot for human beings, used particularly during the summer by yachtsmen for anchoring and landing. Access across the creeks to Stone Point is available but, as with other areas in this locality, it would be unwise for anyone who is unfamiliar with the terrain to attempt it without a degree of planning beforehand.

It was reported after the 'Black Monday' floods of November 1897, which affected much of the south east coastal region, that the Naze itself, of which Stone Marsh is an extension, could once have become an island if it had not been for the vigilance of generations of Walton townsfolk who had taken great pains to ensure that the sea defences were always adequately maintained. The low-lying area of land between the Naze and the adjacent mainland to the south-west used to be known as Walton Gap and even in the 18th century the Essex historian, Philip Morant, noted that because of coastal erosion the Naze was in danger of becoming a island.

After the Great Tide of 1953 it was actually suggested by a group of farmers that Hamford Water, the main channel in the Backwaters, should be dammed completely (along with the Rivers Crouch and Roach further south) to provide greater protection against future flooding, to increase the area of land which could be used for agriculture and to reduce the cost of seawall maintenance. Although this proposal never came to fruition seven creeks around the county were actually dammed during the years following the Great Tide, one of those being Foundry Creek just outside Walton.

The area around Stone Marsh has yielded some important archæological discoveries over the years, particularly of prehistoric flintwork. (It was given the name 'Flint Island' in Arthur Ransome's *Secret Water*.) This includes over 1,000 pressure-flaked arrowheads' which have been found over a two mile length of coast south east of Stone Point. Clacton-on-Sea, several miles down the coast from Walton, is one of the earliest positively identified settlement areas in the country.

RAY ISLAND [Parkeston Quay]

"...a vast project of land reclamation..."
                    LEONARD WEAVER, *Harwich: Gateway to the Continent*

To the north of the Backwaters, across the Harwich peninsular in the River Stour, is the last of the islands on this geographical tour.

Ray Island, apparently named after a former landowner, is now technically no longer an island at all, as it has been absorbed into the mainland by the reclamation of land to the west. Ramsey Creek, which emerges in the Stour to the east of the island, is still there, but is a little hidden from view.

The island's main claim to fame is as the home of Parkeston Quay - a major departure point for ships to Holland and other overseas destinations - and the whole island is dominated by commercial activities, ranging from those associated with the port and docks to others at the nearby oil refinery and storage depôt. Nevertheless, there is, perhaps surprisingly, some residential occupation, with half a dozen streets of houses south of the port, including churches, a post office and a pub. There is also a golf course at Ray Farm.

The story of the modern development of Ray Island begins in the late 19th century with the Great Eastern Railway (G.E.R.) which found that the facilities for handling its steamers at Harwich were becoming inadequate and decided to develop its own quay a couple of miles upstream. Harwich townsfolk were not particularly pleased with this decision but could do little about it. The new quay at Ray Island, named Parkeston Quay after the G.E.R.'s chairman, Charles Henry Parkes, soon grew rapidly and Harwich was left behind. Only the Navy Yard and a Trinity House depôt remained.

Six hundred acres of land were developed at Parkeston to see the scheme through and a two-and-a-half mile long embankment was constructed around Ray Island, enabling seven ships to be accommodated simultaneously at the new 1,800-feet long quay. All this activity led in turn to the development of a separate self-supporting community at Parkeston which was soon boasting hotel and custom house facilities and its own railway station. There was also a brickworks and a school for the children of the families of the new Parkeston community. Ray is a deceptively high island and some of the streets - most of which are named after local people involved with the original development of Parkeston Quay - are surprisingly steep.

This was not the first engineering scheme to be proposed for the area in the Victorian period, though most of the previous schemes had been aimed at

The gateway to Parkestone Quay at Ray Island

'The Captain Fryatt', Ray Island

the shallow but extensive mile-wide bay area between Harwich Bathside and the shores of Ray Island.  From 1845 onwards a whole range of schemes for dockland developments there was published, most of them being far too ambitious ever to have a hope of getting off the ground.  An Act of Parliament supporting one of the schemes was actually passed in 1853 but little came of it.  The G.E.R. ultimately opted for the development of Ray Island in the 1870s in preference to Bathside because it was a cheaper and more practical option where ships of a larger draught could far more easily be accommodated.

Plans for reclamation of the bay between Bath Side and Ray Island continued to be drawn up into the first decade of this century, but the unfailing success of Parkeston invalidated most of them before they had even been published.  In recent years there has finally been some development at Bath Side, though on a much smaller scale than envisaged by the Victorians.  A new road bypass around Dovercourt to Harwich old town has opened up the land there, a new supermarket has been built and other retail park developments are planned.  In Parkeston itself a new formal garden area looks set to be created.

Harwich is evidently thriving and most of the thousands of people who travel abroad from the town every year are blissfully unaware that this is because of the rôle that Ray Island - an island they unwittingly pass over on their way to Parkeston Quay - has played in the development of new port facilities.  Similarly, visitors from abroad,  setting foot in the country for the first time, will also largely be unaware that the soil they are standing on belongs to one of Essex's many fascinating islands.

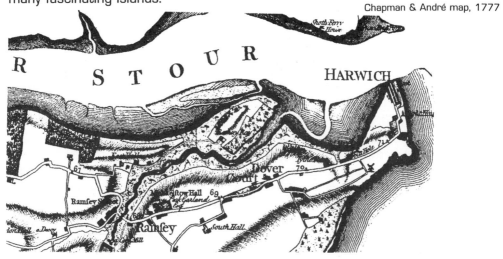

Chapman & André map, 1777

## THE JOURNEY ENDS

*"A monument to human perseverance..."*

HILDA GRIEVE, *The Great Tide*

For the purposes of this book our trip around the county's shoreline has reached its end, but it should be apparent from the journey that there is much of interest in Essex's numerous islands.

It should also be apparent that a similar trip in a hundred years or so may well throw up a number of new islets or identify the disappearance of some of today's more familiar islands. Brightlingsea, for example, indisputably mainland now, was once an island, while the area around Brick House Farm, near Mundon, on the southern shore of the River Blackwater, was also once surrounded by water. Conversely, Buxey Sandbank, in the waters off Dengie Hundred, was once a rich grazing ground, covered with trees.

The way of life on an island remains precarious. The sea is constantly trying to reclaim what it has lost or to take anew mainland areas which it has never yet owned. More and more flood defences, including the great tidal barrier in the River Thames at Woolwich, have been introduced to repel the waters, but how effective can they ever really be? The past 300 years have seen storm after storm, tidal surge after tidal surge, threatening a growing number of island inhabitants and on each occasion the devastation caused by these attacks has been recorded as the "worst ever". In the 20th century alone there were significantly high tides recorded in (amongst others) the years 1928, 1938, 1949, 1953, 1978, 1987, 1990 and 1993 on the east coast. In the worst inundation in recent history, the Great Tide of 1953, which was perhaps genuinely the worst ever flooding incident in Essex, almost 21,000 people in the county were made homeless. Over half of these lived on islands. A further 119 people lost their lives in Essex during the inundation - more than a third of the whole toll for the east coast. Again, over half of these fatalities took place on the county's islands. Can things really go on getting 'worse'?

As recently as February, 1993, a freak tide on the east coast caused £1.2 million worth of damage to defensive seawalls, £130,000 of this cost being incurred by bills for repairs to Essex flood defences. The Strood access road to Mersea Island was cut off for hours and regions on the banks of the River Blackwater suffered substantial flooding. The flood defence authorities are doing sterling work, but with the advent of global warming, how much more of the county's rich agricultural, residential and recreational coastal and island

land will be lost to the sea in the next hundred years?

For some this begs the question as to whether island life will ever be truly viable. For others, of course, notably those who actually live on the islands, there can be no other way of life. On Canvey and Mersea and Foulness generations of islanders have survived between them the effects of floods, earthquakes, attacks by enemy aircraft and weapons testing exercises, applications for huge residential developments and schemes for airports which would have devastated their homes and livelihoods, and centuries of gradual, natural coastal erosion. No-one will ever move them, so Life goes on.

You have seen, I hope, in this work something which has given you an indication of what the greatest county for islands on the east coast of this country has to offer. Be it natural landscapes, fascinating histories or seaside souvenirs that you seek, look closely and you will find it here.

Island Lane, Kirby-le-Soken, leading to Horsey Island

# BIBLIOGRAPHY

The following books were very useful to the author during his research:

Angell, Sir Norman, *After all*, Hamish Hamilton, 1951

Astbury, A.K., *Estuary*, Carnforth Press, 1980

Baldwin, William, *Early recollections at Great Oakley*, 1983

Baldwin,William, *Further reminiscences of happenings at Bramble Island over past years*, 1983

Baring-Gould, Sabine, *Mehalah*, Smith Elder, 1880

Barnes, Alison, *Essex Eccentrics*, Essex Libraries, 1987

Barsby, Geoff, *Canvey Island*, Phillimore, 1992

Barsby, Geoff, *Canvey Island*, Tempus Publishing, 1997

Beckett, Reginald A., *Romantic Essex*, Dent, 1901

Benham, Hervey, *The last stronghold of sail*, Harrap, 1948

Benton, Philip, *The history of Rochford Hundred*, Harrington, 1888

Booker, John, *Essex and the Industrial Revolution*, Essex County Council, 1974

Bowskill, Derek, *The East Coast*, Imray Laurie Norie & Wilson, 1984

Buckley D.G. (Ed.), *Archæology in Essex to A.D. 1500*, The Council for British Archæology, 1980

Clarke, Peter & Margaret, *Where to watch birds in East Anglia*, A. & C. Black, 1988

Clarke, Vernon, *Walking the seawalls of Essex*, Vernon Clarke, 1983

Colchester Archæological Group, *The Red Hills of Essex*, Colchester Archæological Group,1990

Coote, Jack H., *East Coast rivers from the air*, Yachting Monthly, 1986 & 1991  (both collections)

Corke, David, *The nature of Essex*, Barracuda Books, 1984

Cracknell, Basil E., *Portrait of London River*, Robert Hale, 1980

Crouch, Marcus, *Essex*, Batsford, 1969

DERA, *Draft Site Management Statement - Foulness SSSI*, 1997

Dobson, John S., *'Fowlness' - the mystery isle, 1914-1939*, Baron,1996

Edgson, Vivien Mary, *A study of Mersea Island to 1970*, Vivien M. Wren, 1993

Edwards, A.C., *A history of Essex*, Phillimore, 1985

Environment Agency leaflets (various)

Essex Wildlife Trust, *A guide to Reserves*, Essex Wildlife Trust, 1987

Evans, H. Muir, *A short history of the Thames Estuary*, Imray Laurie Norie & Wilson, c. 1925

Federation of Women's Institutes, *The Essex village book*, Countryside Books,1988

Ford, Peter, *Tendring Peninsula*, Ian Henry Publications, 1988

Gifford, P R. (Ed.), *Resist the invader*, Essex Libraries, 1982

Grieve, Hilda, *The Great Tide*, Essex County Council, 1959

Griffiths, Maurice, *The first of the Tide*, Conway Maritime Press, 1979

Gunton, Tony, *Discovering the Essex Countryside*, Essex Wildlife Trust, 1994

Harland, M. & H., *The flooding of Eastern England*, Minimax Books, 1980

Health and Safety Executive, *Canvey: a second report*, Health & Safety Executive, 1981

Health and Safety Executive, *The Canvey Report*, Health & Safety Executive, 1978

Helliwell, Leonard (Ed.), *South East Essex in the Saxon Period*, Museums Publications, 1971

Herbert, A.P., *The Thames*, Weidenfield & Nicolson, 1966

Hough, John, *Essex Churches*, Boydell Press, 1983

*Island Times* (various issues)

Jarvis, Stan, *Essex*, Shire Publications, 1986

Jerram-Burrows, Lily, *The smaller islands of the River Crouch*, Rochford Hundred Historical Society, 1980

Kent, Peter, *Fortifications of East Anglia*, Terence Dalton, 1988

Maldon District Council, *Northey Island*, Maldon District Council, 1991

Manning, S. A., *Portrait of Essex*, Robert Hale, 1977

Manton, J. S., *Potton Island - past & present*, 1939

McCave, Fred, *A history of Canvey Island*, Ian Henry Publications, 1985

McCave, Fred, *Canvey Island in old picture postcards*, European Library, 1987

Mee, Arthur, *The King's England - Essex*, Hodder & Stoughton, 1942

Meteorological Office, *The Storm Tide Forecasting Service*, Meteorological Office, 1999

Minutes of the Emergency Planning Meeting, 19th November, 1996, The Paddocks, Canvey Island

Morant, Philip, *The history and antiquities of the County of Essex*, 1768 [Reprinted 1978 by EP Publishing]

Morgan, Glyn, *Secret Essex*, Ian Henry Publications, 1982

Morgan, Glyn, *The romance of Essex inns*, Ian Henry Publications, 1983

Morgan, Glyn, *The romance of Thameside taverns*, Essex Countryside, 1967

National Trust, *Northey Island*, 1991

Neale, Kenneth, *Essex in history*, Phillimore, 1977

Ogley, Bob & Reynolds, Kev, *Eye on the hurricane*, Froglets Publications, 1989

Payne, Jessie, *A ghost hunter's guide to Essex*, Ian Henry Publications, 1987

Pevsner, Nikolaus, *The Buildings of England - Essex*, Penguin, 1988 (reprint)

Pluckwell, George, *Smuggling villages of North East Essex*, Ian Henry Publications, 1986

Quarrell, Johnnie, *Portrait of Foulness*, Ian Henry Publications, 1998

Ransome, Arthur, *Secret Water*, Jonathan Cape, 1939

Reaney, P.H. *The place-names of Essex*, Cambridge University Press, 1969

Rochford District Council, *Rochford - our heritage, our future*, Rochford District Council, undated

Rodwell, Warwick, *South East Essex in the Roman Period*, County Borough of Southend-on-Sea, 1971

Scarfe, Norman, *Essex*, Faber, 1975

Scott, E.V. (compiler), *The best of Essex*, Egon Publishers, 1988

Shrapnel, Norman, *A view of the Thames*, Collins, 1977

Smith, Charlotte Fell (Ed.), *An anthology of Essex*, Sampson Low Marston, 1911

Smith, J R., *Foulness*, Essex Record Office, 1970

Smith, J R., *Maldon*, Maldon Corporation, 1971

Smith, Victor, *Defending London's River*, North Kent Books, 1985

Strugnell, Kenneth W., *Seagates to the Saxon Shore*, Terence Dalton, 1973

Thames Estuary Conservation Group, *The Thames Estuary*, Thames Estuary Conservation Group, 1983

Walker, Leonard, *Background to Domesday*, Leonard Walker, 1988

Weaver, David, *Essex tales*, Ian Henry Publications, 1985

Weaver, Leonard, *Harwich - gateway to the Continent*, Terence Dalton, 1990

Wentworth Day, James, *Coastal adventure*, Harrap, 1949

Wentworth Day, James, *Farming adventure*, Harrap, 1943

Whitcomb, Olivia, *Invaders of Canvey*, Essex Libraries, 1982

Witheridge, Janet, *History of the hulks on Northey Island*, 1999

Woodward & Cockerill, *The siege of Colchester*, Essex Libraries, 1979

Yearsley, Ian, *Essex events*, Phillimore., 1999

Yearsley, Ian, *Water towers in Essex*, manuscript, 1989

Additional material was gathered from *Essex Countryside* magazine, local newspapers, Essex parish church guidebooks, company histories, museum leaflets and local authority tourist publications.

Skipper's Island Lodge